I0820641

One NATION *Under God*

40 DEVOTIONS FOR PATRIOTIC WOMEN

AMANDA C. BAUCH

A POST HILL PRESS BOOK

One Nation Under God:
40 Devotions for Patriotic Women

ISBN: 979-8-89565-111-7
ISBN (eBook): 979-8-89565-112-4

Cover design by Conroy Accord
Interior design by Greg Johnson, Textbook Perfect

Post Hill Press
New York • Nashville
posthillpress.com

Published in the United States of America
1 2 3 4 5 6 7 8 9 10

To my Lord and Savior Jesus Christ

Source Credits for Hymn Lyrics

"Before You, Lord, We Bow," stanza 2. Lyrics by Francis Scott Key. Public Domain Use.

"Dearest Jesus, We Are Here," stanza 5. Lyrics by Benjamin Schmolck. Translated by Catherine Winkworth. Public Domain Use.

"God Bless Our Native Land." Lyrics by Charles T. Brooks (stanza 1) and John S. Dwight (stanza 2). Public Domain Use.

"If God Himself Be for Me," stanza 8. Lyrics by Paul Gerhardt. Translated by Richard Massie. Public Domain Use.

"Hail to the Lord's Anointed," stanza 4. Lyrics by James Montgomery. Public Domain Use.

"O Come, O Come, Emmanuel," stanza 7. Latin, c. 12th century. *Psalteriolum Cantionum Catholicarum*. Translated by John Mason Neale. Public Domain Use.

"O Lord, How Shall I Meet You," stanza 6. Lyrics by Paul Gerhardt. Translated by Catherine Winkworth. Public Domain Use.

"Lord, Keep Us Steadfast in Your Word," stanza 3. Lyrics by Martin Luther. Translated by Catherine Winkworth. Public Domain Use.

"The People That in Darkness Sat," stanza 5. Lyrics by John Morison. Public Domain Use.

"When in the Hour of Deepest Need," stanza 3. Lyrics by Paul Eber. Translated by Catherine Winkworth. Public Domain Use.

Contents

Author's Note

When I originally conceived the idea for this book, I was thinking in much broader terms. I wanted to write something that would glorify God and edify the body of Christ, in the context of encouraging and equipping readers to pray for the United States.

However, once I started writing, something became clear to me. I wasn't writing for any and all believers in this country—I was speaking specifically to Christian *women*. The moms who worry about the way social media and a sexualized culture are affecting their children. The young women who are concerned about their personal safety and their futures. The grandmothers who don't recognize the country in which they raised their own children and want better for their grandchildren and great-grandchildren.

I've had many conversations with women, particularly in the past few years, who have expressed fears and despair over the state of our nation. Even so, these conversations have always been infused with *hope*. Hope that our country can turn things around and that we can be a part of turning the tide, starting with our own families. And the hope we have in our Lord and Savior Jesus Christ, who reigns over heaven and earth.

May this book inspire Christian women to apply God's wisdom to the challenges we face and the opportunities we have in the United States. My prayer is that it will indeed edify the body of Christ and glorify God, "who is and who was and who is to come" (Revelation 1:4).

Introduction

Tears streamed down my face as I slowly read through the day's headlines on my phone. It seemed that every day, the more I scrolled, the worse I felt.

Once in a while, a news site I frequented would post a positive or inspirational story, but those were few and far between. Nevertheless, each day I sifted through stories of war, murder, suicide, violence, and political mudslinging, like a prospector shaking a tray to find an elusive golden nugget of good news.

To me, some of the most distressing news concerned events in the United States. As someone who was raised in a military family, love for this great nation has been instilled within me. We had Flag Day concerts in elementary school, where we proudly waved tiny American flags throughout the program. We had Fourth of July and Memorial Day parades, where Scouts rode bikes, drill teams twirled rifles, and marching bands performed. (I have intimate experience because I was part of the latter two groups.) At these and many other events in my small town in Southwestern New York, veterans were always a centerpiece, as we honored their service and sacrifice.

Back then, I had no way of knowing that the country I loved—and still fiercely love and would give my life for—would one day appear to be coming apart at the seams. Hence my tears at reading the daily headlines.

I cried out, "God, what is happening in this country? Everything is going off the rails, and the news seems worse every day. What can we do—what can *I* do—in the face of all this hatred and violence?"

One of my greatest flaws as a Christian, and as a person, is that I am a *horrible* listener. When I pray, I often don't wait for a response. I typically say or write, "Amen!" and scurry along to whatever's next on my agenda.

But that day, I sat in silence after sending up my desperate plea. I took deep, calming breaths until my nerves and mind were soothed, and wiped away my subsiding tears. As I sat there in the silent stillness, the clear, simple answer drifted into my mind: *pray.*

My eyes widened, and I couldn't help but laugh.

For almost twenty years now, I've had a running joke with God. I cry out to Him, asking what to do. And the answer is the same: *pray.* You'd think that by now, I'd know this. But if life has taught me anything, it's that I'm about as stiff-necked and stubborn as they come.

In spite of two decades of my questions being answered with *pray*, it still surprised me on this day. I'm not sure why, though. Did the problems America and the world were facing seem too big, the animosity too deep-seated? Or was I forgetting the thing that I always seem to forget: *Prayer is the single most powerful weapon we have in our arsenal against the dark and evil forces in our world.*

Even though we Christians disagree on many things, I think we can all agree that prayer is powerful.

After I was reminded to pray, another thought occurred to me: What if every Christian in the United States committed to praying for our nation each day for an entire year? What miracles could be wrought if we fell to our knees and bowed our heads for 365 days, faithfully lifting up our government, institutions, leaders, and citizens to the Lord's throne of grace and mercy?

The Bible contains numerous instances of intercessory prayer (for a small sampling, see Genesis 18:22–33; Exodus 32:9–14; Daniel 9:3–19; and Luke 23:34). Although God is omniscient and omnipotent, He loves hearing from His children and granting those petitions that align with His will.

Honestly, even if we all pray every day for a year, America might not change. In fact, things might get even worse. I say that not to discourage or serve as a deterrent, but as a statement of fact and a hard truth of the reality of living in a sinful world. As we know from the fall of ancient Israel, sometimes a nation and a people pass a point of no return. And the Lord, in His justice, must enact punishment. Yet the faithful remnant of the Israelites was eventually restored to its land, albeit in absence of the former glory and with much heartache.

However, even if nothing changes in our country, *we* will be changed. Come what may, we'll be better equipped to navigate our chaotic world, until the Lord calls us home or Jesus Christ returns. We will be able to persevere, for the Spirit of the Lord who dwells within us will continually remind us that our Lord and Savior Jesus Christ has already overcome the world (John 16:33).

Won't you join me in praying for our country every day? We have nothing to lose, and everything to gain, for "the effective, fervent prayer of a righteous man avails much" (James 5:16).

How to Use This Devotional

I love devotional books, journaling (including writing down prayers), and Scripture. In this book, I've combined these loves, providing a Bible reading, a brief meditation, a prayer prompt, questions for further reflection, and a place for you to note your thoughts, your prayers, your doodles—however you want to fill that space.

I'd also like to note that the Bible passages and verses I've used as the focal point for each devotion are by no means an exhaustive representation of what God's Word says about the topics discussed. I had many other verses I could have used—and believe me, I struggled to whittle my original list down to forty! But these are the ones I settled on for this book.

This book contains forty devotionals. The number forty has significance, and it's woven throughout the Bible. In general, it represents a period of trial and testing. It rained forty days and nights during the Great Flood. The Israelites wandered through the wilderness for forty years. Jesus entered the wilderness and fasted for forty days and nights before Satan came and tempted Him. After Jesus's resurrection, He appeared visibly on earth for forty days until His ascension. And these are only a few examples of the times the number forty is used in the Bible.

You may consider reading one entry a week, or you might prefer to read one per day. Perhaps you'll incorporate the devotional into a seasonal practice, such as reading one entry per day during Lent. Or you might read the book with a group, using your answers to the reflection questions as the basis for your discussion. I know from experience what a blessing it is when women gather around Scripture together!

In short, I encourage you to use this book in whatever way works best for you.

One thing I've always struggled with in my prayer life is *consistency*. Whenever I want to implement a new habit, whether it's for my physical health, to meet a goal, or for a spiritual discipline, I might be able to sustain the effort for a few weeks, even for several months. But doing something every day, *for an entire year*? Not so much. Yet as the old saying goes, let's not allow the perfect to become the enemy of the good. The last thing Satan wants anyone doing is praying—especially praying consistently and with intentionality. Even if all we're able to offer on any given day is a prayer whispered on a deep exhale of sadness, that is still a fragrant offering to the Lord (see Romans 8:26 and Psalm 141:2).

In my years of spending time in God's Word, one truth has been continually reinforced to me: His Word is indeed living and active (Hebrews 4:12)! Therefore, even when we encounter the same Bible passage multiple times, it is never the same twice. One reason is that we receive fresh insights from the Holy

Spirit. Another reason is that we are dynamic human beings, ever becoming the people God created us to be. I've had days when I read a Bible verse in the morning, then lived what felt like a bazillion lifetimes in one day, and read the same verse in the evening with a completely different perspective or understanding. Not saying this happens each and every time, but for me at least, it happens more often than not.

The critical thing is to set an intention to pray for America every day, and do everything within your power to make good on that promise. Our nation needs prayer *now*.

I'm so grateful to have you joining me on this journey, and to have you as a sister in Christ. Together we are stronger, by the power of the Holy Spirit that unites us in the body of Christ. To Him be all glory and honor, forever and ever. Amen.

God bless our native land;
Firm may she ever stand
Through storm and night,
When the wild tempests rave,
Ruler of wind and wave,
Do Thou our country save
By Thy great might.
So shall our prayers arise
To God above the skies;
On Him we wait.
Thou who art ever nigh,
Guarding with watchful eye,
To thee aloud we cry:
God save the state!

"God Bless Our Native Land"

In the Beginning

In the beginning God created the heavens and the earth. The earth was without form, and void; and darkness was on the face of the deep. And the Spirit of God was hovering over the face of the waters.

Then God said, "Let there be light"; and there was light. And God saw the light, that it was good; and God divided the light from the darkness. God called the light Day, and the darkness He called Night. So the evening and the morning were the first day.

—GENESIS 1:1–5

Does your life ever feel chaotic? Does the entire world seem chaotic to you?

If you spend even one minute on the internet, you'll likely start thinking like Chicken Little, convinced that the sky is falling.

School shootings. Child trafficking. Suicide bombings. Wars and more wars.

Yet the world was never meant to be this way.

"In the beginning God" is an awesome statement, revealing that before anything *was*—even time and space—God *is*. He is the great "I AM," the unique and singular name He revealed to Moses in Exodus 3:14, sometimes translated from the Hebrew as "Yahweh." His very name conveys His dominion over all, as

He is the only one who can create *ex nihilo*, meaning bringing something into existence from nothing. By His will and word, the world was brought into being.

We also read that "the Spirit of God was hovering over the face of the waters." The opening verses of the Bible assert the truth of the Trinity, even though the word itself is never explicitly used in Scripture. Like the Father, the Spirit is uncreated, yet He acted in creation. The same is true of the Son, who is uncreated and acted in creation.

In the beginning, "the earth was without form, and void; and darkness was on the face of the deep." From the first day of creation through the subsequent five days, the Lord methodically brought all things into being. We worship a God of order, not of chaos (see 1 Corinthians 14:33).

At the end of every single day, God proclaimed that what He'd created was good. He alone defines what is "good" and "evil," though humanity often tries to obscure His absolute truth with relative truths, as we often see in today's culture. It's the age-old sin of questioning God's love and goodness and the truth of His Word, of asking, as the serpent did in the Garden of Eden, "Has God indeed said...?" (Genesis 3:1).

In God's absence, darkness and chaos abound, and life does feel like a void without form. We can see this in both our individual lives and in our nation. When we look around our country, God's absence in every sphere of society manifests in the ills that plague us. Those of us who have been unbelievers—or even those of us who have drifted away from the Lord for a season—know what it's like to live as an enemy of God, severed from His love, grace, and mercy.

For those who are in the body of Christ, God's sovereignty in creation is a powerful reminder that even in moments of chaos and uncertainty in our lives—and in our country—He can bring forth order. He also can bring forth light from the darkness, which He did on the very first day of creation, when He said, "Let there be light."

These opening verses in the Bible point us to Jesus, "the light of the world" (John 8:12). This is reinforced by John 1:1–5, which beautifully echoes Genesis 1:1–4: "In the beginning was the Word, and the Word was with God, and the Word was God. He was in the beginning with God. All things were made through Him, and without Him nothing was made that was made. In Him was life, and the life was the light of men. And the light shines in the darkness, and the darkness did not comprehend it."

The Word was with the Father from eternity, attesting to their unity even after He became flesh, when He proclaimed, "I and My Father are one" and "before Abraham was, I AM" (John 10:30, 8:58). As John 1:3 states, nothing was made apart from the Word, and He is the one who is "upholding all things by the word of His power" (Hebrews 1:3).

Even before anything was created, God, in His omniscience, knew that humanity would fall into sin. Because He loves us and doesn't want anyone to perish (2 Peter 3:9; Ezekiel 18:23), the salvation plan was established before Adam was formed from the dust of the ground and the breath of life was breathed into his nostrils (Genesis 2:7). As Revelation 13:8 says, Jesus Christ is "the Lamb slain from the foundation of the world."

Acknowledging the Triune God's dominion and sovereignty over all creation should inspire us to worship, as we not only admire the beauty and wonder that surrounds us but also honor the One who created it with such intentionality and love—and the One who redeemed it by shedding His blood on the cross.

We eagerly anticipate Christ's return, when the things of this world will pass away, and He'll make all things new (Revelation 21:5).

Prayer

Lord of all creation, when we look around us, Your might and majesty are evident in creation. From the stars in the heavens to the depths of the seas, You uphold all things—including our nation. As we spend the coming weeks lifting up our nation in prayer, may we humble ourselves and continually remember that the earth is Yours, the world and all those who dwell in it (Psalm 24:1). In Jesus's name we pray. Amen.

For Further Reflection

- Some people believe that God created the world, set it in motion, and left human beings to fend for themselves. Does Scripture support this idea? Other than the creation narrative, do additional Bible verses provide insight on this topic?
- How does the knowledge that God created everything, both seen and unseen, affect your understanding of His power over all things, including nations and governments?

Prayer That Avails Much

Confess your trespasses to one another, and pray for one another, that you may be healed. The effective, fervent prayer of a righteous man avails much. Elijah was a man with a nature like ours, and he prayed earnestly that it would not rain; and it did not rain on the land for three years and six months. And he prayed again, and the heaven gave rain, and the earth produced its fruit.

—JAMES 5:16–18

Our Father, who art in heaven...

Did I reply to that email? I'm pretty sure I did.... I'll just grab my phone and check quickly...

No! You're supposed to be praying. Focus!

Hallowed be Thy name...

Wait—am I picking up the kids from school today...?

Does your prayer time ever sound like this?

Mine sometimes does, and way more often than I'd care to admit.

Maybe we don't pray daily, or our prayers are perfunctory—something to be checked off the to-do list before we move on to the next thing. Or perhaps we think we don't know how to pray or what to pray for, or we worry that we're not "good enough" for God to listen to us.

Christians are in a spiritual battle. The world hates us and wants to destroy us, as well as everything that is good and godly—children and unborn babies, marriage and families, peace and prosperity, among other blessings from the Lord.

While fighting this battle, we sometimes struggle to wield one of the most powerful weapons in our arsenal: prayer.

James says that "the effective, fervent prayer of a righteous man avails much." But what is an "effective, fervent" prayer?

The effective prayer is one offered in faith, confidence, and trust that the Lord of the universe wants to hear from us and does hear us. As Jesus instructs in Matthew 7:7: "Ask, and it will be given to you; seek, and you will find; knock, and it will be opened to you."

Prayer is about being in fellowship and having a conversation with God.

Think of it this way: If a husband and wife never talk to one another, will their marriage be strong? Or what if the husband only speaks to his wife when he needs something, or the wife only speaks to her husband when she wants to complain?

Consider your answers to those questions in the context of talking to God. What does your prayer life say about your fellowship with Him?

The fervent prayer is one that's beyond "one and done"—it's persistent and never gives up. Have you ever seen a child begging her father for something? Picture it: The child clings to the father, wrapping her arms around dad's leg or tugging on dad's hand. She looks up at her father with wide, pleading eyes.

She might say over and over again, "Please, Daddy, please please please?" That is a visual image of a fervent prayer.

The notion that the prayer must be from a "righteous man" might throw us for a loop. We might wonder if we're "righteous" enough for our prayers to "avail much." This is where the beauty of the Gospel shines. Our righteousness doesn't depend on us—what we do or how we feel—because sin taints our actions and feelings. Our righteousness depends on one thing, and one thing only: the complete and sufficient work of Jesus Christ on the cross.

Since Jesus is our Savior, we're clothed in His righteousness. So when we offer a prayer in faith, that prayer holds infinite power—power from the One who created the universe and still holds it all together.

A prayer also is effective when we seek God's will, not our own. When we align ourselves with the Father's will, our prayers can move mountains, because with God, all things are possible (Matthew 19:26). And even when we don't see any immediate results from our prayers, we can trust that God's will is being done in and through them.

To better understand this, we need look no further than James 5:16–18, with Elijah as an example of how the "effective, fervent prayer of a righteous man avails much." Elijah was an Old Testament prophet, who spoke on God's behalf when wicked King Ahab ruled the Northern Kingdom of Israel.

As James mentions, Elijah prayed earnestly that it wouldn't rain for three years and six months. The Lord had warned His people about this specific punishment, in Deuteronomy 11:16–17:

"Take heed to yourselves, lest your heart be deceived, and you turn aside and serve other gods and worship them, lest the Lord's anger be aroused against you, and He shut up the heavens so that there be no rain, and the land yield no produce, and you perish quickly from the good land which the Lord is giving you."

Because the people had turned aside and served other gods, Elijah prayed that the One True God would uphold this punishment. In this way, his will aligned with God's will. Thus, it didn't rain for three years and six months.

Then, in 1 Kings 18:41–46, when Elijah prayed for the drought to be lifted, the Lord once again heeded Elijah's prayer, and it rained.

It's easy to look at someone like Elijah and think, *Of course God heard his prayers and granted his requests! He was a mighty prophet who even put his life on the line to obey and serve the Lord!* Yet James dispels this idea when he says, "Elijah was a man with a nature like ours." Elijah was just as human and just as much of a sinner in need of a Savior as the rest of us. However, this man who was made righteous by God prayed effective, fervent prayers that impacted an entire nation, because they were aligned with God's will.

Psalm 18:6 says, "In my distress I called upon the Lord, and cried out to my God; He heard my voice from His temple, and my cry came before Him, even to His ears." We, too, can be like Elijah and pray transformative, intercessory prayers on behalf of America, seeking His will for us. As appropriate, we can ask the Lord to withhold blessing from our nation, to lead people to repent and seek the Lord. And we can ask Him to heal and bless our nation, that His name may be honored and glorified.

Prayer

Jesus, You tell us that even if our faith is as small as a mustard seed, nothing will be impossible for us (Matthew 17:20). Please help us to be like Elijah, so we have complete confidence that You hear us when we call on You and trust that You're mighty enough to do whatever we ask. As we lift up our nation in prayer in the coming days, allow our will for this country and its people to align with Your will for us. Amen.

For Further Reflection

- How can you make "effective, fervent" prayer a part of your daily life? What might you need to give up to make that a reality?
- What specific prayer concerns do you have for the United States? Make a list, and start lifting those petitions to the Lord, every day! As you read through this devotional, you might find even more requests to add to your list.

____

____

____

____

____

____

____

____

Be Careful What You Ask For

"And you will cry out in that day because of your king whom you have chosen for yourselves, and the Lord will not hear you in that day."
Nevertheless the people refused to obey the voice of Samuel; and they said, "No, but we will have a king over us, that we also may be like all the nations, and that our king may judge us and go out before us and fight our battles."
And Samuel heard all the words of the people, and he repeated them in the hearing of the Lord. So the Lord said to Samuel, "Heed their voice, and make them a king."

—1 SAMUEL 8:18–22

Sometimes God lets us have our way, even when it's to our own detriment.

That was certainly true of the Israelites when God allowed them to have a king other than Him.

Until that time, the Lord Himself had been their ruler. He'd parted the Red Sea for them. He'd rained down manna for sustenance during the forty years they wandered in the wilderness. He'd gone before them into the Promised Land, giving them miraculous victories that allowed them to claim their inheritance from Him. And He'd provided them with judges, such as Samuel, to lead them.

Yet none of this was good enough for them.

They said, "We will have a king over us, that we also may be like all the nations, and that our king may judge us and go out before us and fight our battles." In spite of God's faithful lordship for about four hundred years, they rejected Him and His rule, instead demanding an earthly king that would offer them a type of security, strength, and identity similar to the surrounding nations. The Lord had set them apart as His chosen people. In rejecting Him, they also rejected this unique, special identity and the blessings that came with it.

The Lord Himself warned them of their folly. He not only delineated the burdens a king would place on them—for example, levying undue taxes and conscripting their sons to fight in wars—but also told them that their status before Him was being jeopardized: "And you will cry out in that day because of your king whom you have chosen for yourselves, and the Lord will not hear you in that day." God makes it clear that He'll allow them to face the consequences of their own decisions, and when they finally buckle under the king's oppression, He'll no longer hear their cries and deliver them.

He'd done this repeatedly during the time of the judges. In that period of Israel's history, a cycle was established: "The children of Israel again did evil in the sight of the Lord" (Judges 3:7 and others). The Lord's anger burned against them, and He sent enemies to afflict them. Each time, "the children of Israel cried out to the Lord," and He sent judges to deliver them (Judges 3:9 and others).

It can be easy for us to scoff at the Israelites. We might think, *If* I'd *seen the wonders the Lord did—the parting of the Red Sea, the walls of Jericho falling, Gideon's victory in battle—I* never *would've rejected Him!*

But are we all that different? Aren't there times when we, too, sinfully trust in our leaders and government to meet our needs? When we feel that if a certain person gets elected or a specific law gets passed, somehow that will move us closer to living in a more "perfect" nation? Or when we believe that solutions to our problems ultimately rest in human activities?

If today's passage from 1 Samuel teaches us nothing else, it should remind us that no good ever comes from elevating earthly authorities and institutions over our sovereign Lord—from placing our trust in sinful, fallible man instead of the sinless, infallible Lord.

In granting the Israelites' request to have a king, with His foreknowledge that it would be a disaster in both the short and long term, the merciful Lord already had a plan in place.

He course corrected the Israelites' sin by establishing a line of kings through David, promising that one day, the Messiah would come from David's progeny (2 Samuel 7:12–16). From Solomon onward, the Israelites wondered, *Is this the One?* Yet each subsequent king proved to be a sinner who fell short. The bad kings far outnumbered the good kings, and the Bible tells us that many of them "did evil in the sight of the Lord," exactly as their fathers before them had done (see 2 Kings 21:2, 20, for example).

No, none of these kings would deliver Israel. And none of our earthly rulers can deliver us (Psalm 146:3).

But one day, many centuries later, the Lord's promise was fulfilled, as we read at the beginning of Matthew's Gospel: "The book of the genealogy of Jesus Christ, the Son of David, the Son of Abraham" (Matthew 1:1). Jesus Christ, King of kings and Lord of lords, is the eternal, perfect King who reigns on His throne both now and forevermore. He "loved us and washed us from our sins in His own blood, and has made us kings and priests to His God and Father" (Revelation 1:5–6). When we trust in Him and His redeeming blood, no matter what happens in our personal lives or in our nation, we can be assured that "no weapon formed against [us] shall prosper" (Isaiah 54:17).

Instead of seeking our own will for our nation, as the Israelites did, let us seek God's will. While that petition might not produce the results we initially hope for, Scripture promises that "all things work together for good to those who love God, to those who are the called according to His purpose" (Romans 8:28). We can't see the bigger picture, but He does.

Prayer

Sovereign Lord, when we reject Your dominion and authority in our lives and over our nation, we reject You. We repent of the times we've placed our final hope in anything but the blood of Jesus, and we humbly ask You to forgive us this sin. May Your will be done, on earth as it is in heaven. Amen.

For Further Reflection

- Are you dealing with any situations where you're ultimately relying on earthly means, including people or government, instead of on the Lord? If so, repent and seek the Lord's forgiveness, asking Him to give you the wisdom and strength to navigate the situation with His help.
- In what ways do we strive to "be like all the nations," whether in our individual lives or in our society?

His righteous government and pow'r
Shall over all extend;
On judgment and on justice based,
His reign shall have no end,
His reign shall have no end.

"The People That in Darkness Sat"

May God Heal Our Land

If My people who are called by My name will humble themselves, and pray and seek My face, and turn from their wicked ways, then I will hear from heaven, and will forgive their sin and heal their land.

—2 CHRONICLES 7:14

Since its founding in 1776, the United States has experienced unprecedented peace and prosperity. While certain situations and hardships have caused struggle and despair (the Civil War and the Great Depression come to mind), overall, the nation has been blessed.

Yet prosperity and complacency often seem to go hand in hand.

We need look no further than ancient Israel to learn this truth.

Israel had everything going for it. It was led by King Solomon, whose God-given wisdom was renowned throughout the world. When the Lord had asked Solomon what he wanted, the king said, "Now give me wisdom and knowledge, that I may go out and come in before this people; for who can judge this great people of Yours?" (2 Chronicles 1:10). The Lord was pleased with Solomon's request and promised him much more than this: "Wisdom and knowledge are granted to you; and I will give you riches and wealth and honor, such as none of the kings have had who were before you, nor shall any after you have the like" (2 Chronicles 1:12).

And throughout Solomon's reign, the Lord fulfilled His promise.

Economically, Israel thrived, establishing lucrative trade partnerships with many other nations, including with Hiram, king of Tyre, who provided much material and many craftsmen to help build the temple. Israel's fleets sailed the seas, and "once every three years the merchant ships came bringing gold, silver, ivory, apes, and monkeys" (1 Kings 10:22). And when other rulers visited, they brought luxurious gifts. For instance, when the queen of Sheba arrived, to see for herself whether Solomon was as rich and wise as she'd heard, she came with an entourage that included "camels that bore spices, gold in abundance, and precious stones" (2 Chronicles 9:1).

After seeing Solomon's wealth and hearing his wisdom for herself, she proclaimed, "Blessed be the Lord your God, who delighted in you, setting you on His throne to be king for the Lord your God! Because your God has loved Israel, to establish them forever, therefore He made you king over them, to do justice and righteousness" (2 Chronicles 9:8). Everything she saw and heard testified to God's glory—not Solomon's—a humbling reminder that "every good gift and every perfect gift is from above" (James 1:17).

Solomon brokered peace with and subdued the surrounding nations, and the Israelites finally had rest after many decades of ongoing war. Israel's army was mighty, with thousands of chariots and horsemen.

Most importantly, Solomon had built the temple, as God had promised to David: "Behold, a son shall be born to you, who shall be a man of rest; and I will give him rest from all his enemies all around. His name shall be Solomon, for I will give peace and quietness to Israel in his days. He shall build a house for My name, and he shall be My son, and I will be his Father; and I will establish the throne of his kingdom over Israel forever" (1 Chronicles 22:9–10). For the first time, the Israelites would have a permanent house of worship—a place where they were guaranteed the Lord's presence, a place to offer sacrifices and receive forgiveness for their sins.

With all of these abundant blessings during Solomon's forty-year reign, you might think that the king and his subjects would be so grateful to the Lord that they'd worship Him and Him only.

Sadly, that wasn't the case.

As we read in 1 Kings 11, Solomon wed many foreign women—seven hundred, in fact, from the very countries the Lord had told the Israelites not to intermarry with, such as Moab, Ammon, and Edom. These wives led him astray and "turned his heart after other gods; and his heart was not loyal to the Lord his God, as was the heart of his father David" (1 Kings 11:4).

The consequences of Solomon's refusal to heed the Lord in this regard were devastating to both him and the entire nation: "Because you have done this, and have not kept My covenant and My statutes, which I have commanded you, I will surely tear the kingdom away from you and give it to your servant. Nevertheless I will not do it in your days, for the sake of your father David; I will tear it out of the hand of your son. However I will not tear away the whole kingdom; I will give one tribe to your son for the sake of My servant David, and for the sake of Jerusalem which I have chosen" (1 Kings 11:11–13).

Even with all the peace and prosperity, all the wealth and wisdom, Solomon fell away. And in the next generation, all but the tribe of Judah would be stripped from his son, Rehoboam.

However, the Lord is merciful and just. At any time, Solomon could have repented, perhaps changing the course of history. Today's verse tells us exactly what this process looks like—and it's the same process any one of us can undertake.

We can *humble ourselves*, acknowledging that we've allowed our pride and self-reliance to undermine our reliance on the Lord, in His guidance and wisdom. We can *pray*, expressing our dependence on Him and seeking His will for our lives and our country. We can *seek His face*, pursuing an intimate connection with our Creator—the Creator of the entire universe. We can *turn from our wicked ways*, repenting with a truly contrite heart for our sins and confessing that we're only saved through the blood of our Lord and Savior Jesus Christ.

And how will the Lord reciprocate?

He will *hear us from heaven*, bending His ear to listen to the cries of His children (Psalm 116:2). He will *forgive our sins*, casting them "as far as the east is from the west" (Psalm 103:12). And He will *heal our land*.

Regardless of any turmoil and strife we endure as individuals or as a nation, we can always trust that genuine repentance opens the way to restoration.

Of course, as long as we live in a world with sin, any worldly healing received will be temporary. Therefore, we Christians long for and look toward the complete and final healing, when the Lord Jesus Christ returns. At that time, every knee shall bow and tongue confess that He is Lord, and He shall make all things new (Philippians 2:10–11; Revelation 21:5). Come, Lord Jesus!

Prayer

Heavenly Father, we know that we can always trust in the promises found in Your Word. Today, as we pray to You and seek Your face, may we repent of any wickedness in our own hearts and minds, and may our nation turn from any and all of its wicked ways. As we humbly come before Your throne of grace and mercy, we ask that You forgive our sins and heal our land, all for the sake of Your Son, Jesus Christ. In His name we pray. Amen.

For Further Reflection

- What are some of the "wicked ways" that the ancient Israelites needed to turn away from? What are some of the "wicked ways" our nation needs to turn away from?
- Although we're guaranteed to have trouble in this world (John 16:33), in your mind, what would a "healed" nation look like?

Abiding in Christ

Abide in Me, and I in you. As the branch cannot bear fruit of itself, unless it abides in the vine, neither can you, unless you abide in Me.
I am the vine, you are the branches. He who abides in Me, and I in him, bears much fruit; for without Me you can do nothing. If anyone does not abide in Me, he is cast out as a branch and is withered; and they gather them and throw them into the fire, and they are burned. If you abide in Me, and My words abide in you, you will ask what you desire, and it shall be done for you. By this My Father is glorified, that you bear much fruit; so you will be My disciples.

—JOHN 15:4–8

Have you ever deeply pondered what it means to abide in Christ?

In today's passage, Jesus uses the imagery of a vine and branches to illustrate our fellowship with Him. In John 15:1, Jesus refers to Himself as "the true vine." He is the source of all life—everything we need in this age and the next. As branches attached to the vine, we're blessed to receive all the nourishment it provides for us. When we're abiding in Christ, we're sustained in mind, body, and spirit.

This sustenance is particularly critical as we navigate living in a world that has priorities and values that clash with the Lord's priorities and our Christian values. We're called to be in the world but not of the world (John 17:16), yet we must be vigilant in not allowing the world's practices and beliefs to infiltrate our lives and hinder our fellowship with Christ.

When this occurs, the consequences can be devastating, as Jesus describes in John 15:6: "If anyone does not abide in Me, he is cast out as a branch and is withered; and they gather them and throw them into the fire, and they are burned." This is a picture of what life is like when someone is severed from the True Vine, as we "wither" during our time on earth and are also in danger of suffering eternal separation from God.

Jesus describes God the Father as the "vinedresser," saying, "Every branch that bears fruit He prunes, that it may bear more fruit" (John 15:1, 2). The role of a vinedresser is to carefully observe every branch on the vine, tending to each one and doing whatever is necessary to ensure that the branch produces optimal fruit. At times that means fertilizing, sometimes that means leaving it alone, and other times that means pruning.

When we're brought to faith in Jesus Christ, that is a pruning in and of itself, as His blood cleanses us from sin, severing us from the old Adam that dwelled within us: "Therefore, if anyone is in Christ, he is a new creation; old things have passed away; behold, all things have become new" (2 Corinthians 5:17). Yet this isn't the final pruning, as we sin daily and are in constant need of the Divine Vinedresser's tender loving care.

These pruning processes can feel painful when things we love and cling to are snipped away. Perhaps it's a friendship or relationship with someone who doesn't exert a godly influence. Maybe it's a TV show or movie that we justify watching because it only contains "a little bit" of objectionable content. Or perhaps it's a habit that's harmful to our overall well-being. Regardless of what's being removed, our sinful flesh resists as it feels the sharp twinge of the Vinedresser's pruning shears. This often doesn't feel like love to us. Yet as any parent who has had to deprive a child of something that's hindering his or her growth—whether candy, a device, or a friendship—knows, love can involve protecting someone from themselves and their own inclinations.

But we can take heart in knowing the truth that the removal of these obstructions to our growth and maturity in Christ allows us to bear more fruit.

Our sinful, fallen world needs the tangible fruit that Christians bear when we abide in Jesus. It needs our charity and faithful stewardship of our time, talents, and treasures. The soup kitchen needs our volunteer hours to help feed those who would otherwise go without. The pregnancy resource center needs our graphic design skills, so we can create beautiful, eye-catching mailings that promote the work it's doing and encourage others to get involved. Our spouses need us to manage the household budget and coordinate the family's schedule. Our children need us to read bedtime stories and pack lunches. Aging parents need us to take time out of our busy schedules to help them with tasks like grocery shopping and running errands.

In so doing, we fulfill what Jesus proclaimed is the second greatest commandment: to love our neighbor as ourselves (Matthew 22:39).

However, the fruit of God precedes the works of our hands. Galatians 5:22–23 tells us that "the fruit of the Spirit is love, joy, peace, longsuffering, kindness, goodness, faithfulness, gentleness, self-control." Apart from Christ, it's impossible for us to demonstrate these godly qualities, and when we take time to self-reflect, the presence or lack of these qualities in our lives can help us determine whether we're abiding in Christ as He desires. If we do feel anxious, stressed, unkind, quarrelsome, impatient, rude, or self-indulgent, we can repent and find peace in Christ's pardon and promise that He will grant us the fruit of His Spirit.

Of course, the most important work we do is share the Gospel—the loving witness that Jesus Christ died for the sins of all people and freely offers forgiveness to everyone, so all might be reconciled to God and dwell with Him for all eternity. As Jesus said, "By this My Father is glorified, that you bear much fruit; so you will be My disciples" (John 15:8). May our lives and witness bear much fruit, so that the Lord will be glorified in all the earth.

Prayer

Lord Jesus Christ, You invite us to abide with You, to stay deeply connected with You in every area of our lives. Help us to do this, Savior, as we strive to resist the pull of the world and its ways and instead embrace the true life that comes from You. May our lives produce fruit in keeping with repentance, reflecting Your love so that You and the Father are glorified. In Your precious and holy name we pray. Amen.

For Further Reflection

- In what ways do you abide with Jesus? What does your life look like when you're resting in Him? Are there any ways that you can be more proactive and intentional in your fellowship with Him?
- What would our nation look like if those of us who abide in Christ were more visibly active in bearing fruit? What might this demonstrate to non-Christians in our country, or to other nations?

Humility in Leadership

And at the end of the time I, Nebuchadnezzar, lifted my eyes to heaven, and my understanding returned to me; and I blessed the Most High and praised and honored Him who lives forever:
For His dominion is an everlasting dominion,
And His kingdom is from generation to generation.
All the inhabitants of the earth are reputed as nothing;
He does according to His will in the army of heaven
And among the inhabitants of the earth.
No one can restrain His hand
Or say to Him, "What have You done?"

—DANIEL 4:34–35

How long had Nebuchadnezzar been in this desolate place? Had it been days? Months? Years?

He didn't remember the taste of food. Or the feeling of his luxurious robes enveloping him. The sound of laughter.

All he knew was darkness and despair.

The pampered and polished king of a world power, sitting high and regal on his throne, had been transformed into a haggard man whose curved, filthy fingernails and scraggly hair rendered him unrecognizable. A man who tore up handfuls of grass to feast on, his body perpetually damp with dew.

This would remain King Nebuchadnezzar's reality, until he humbled himself before the Lord.

Over a century earlier, the Assyrians had demolished Israel's Northern Kingdom, as numerous prophets had warned would happen (for example, see Isaiah 10:5–6 and Hosea 11:5). Similar prophecies were also made about Judah, particularly by Jeremiah. In one such prophecy, Jeremiah declared: "Therefore thus says the Lord of hosts: 'Because you have not heard My words, behold, I will send and take all the families of the north,' says the Lord, 'and Nebuchadnezzar the king of Babylon, My servant, and will bring them against this land, against its inhabitants, and against these nations all around, and will utterly destroy them, and make them an astonishment, a hissing, and perpetual desolations'" (Jeremiah 25:8–9).

In God's mercy—and because Judah was periodically blessed with kings who served Him—He allowed that kingdom to persist much longer than its northern counterpart. Nevertheless, the judgment had been pronounced, and since the Judahites refused to repent, they, too, were exiled.

Did you notice how the Lord referred to Nebuchadnezzar in the Jeremiah passage? He called him "My servant." That notion might conflict with our ideas of who can be a servant of the Lord. How could such a thing be said of a pagan king, especially by our holy, loving God?

God's purposes are always fulfilled, and periodically, He uses the ungodly to bring them about. Throughout Scripture, we have several examples of pagan rulers whom God used both to execute judgment on His people—such as Nebuchadnezzar—and to bless His people—such as Cyrus, king of Persia. The ultimate goal of these punishments is always to lead people back to Him, if only they repent.

In the case of Nebuchadnezzar, he destroyed the kingdom of Judah and ransacked Jerusalem: "And all the articles from the house of God, great and small, the treasures of the house of the Lord, and the treasures of the king and of his leaders, all these he took to Babylon. Then they burned the house of God, broke down the wall of Jerusalem, burned all its palaces with fire, and destroyed all its precious possessions. And those who escaped from the sword he carried away to Babylon, where they became servants to him and his sons until the rule of the kingdom of Persia, to fulfill the word of the Lord by the mouth of Jeremiah" (2 Chronicles 36:18–21).

For the Israelites, nothing was more devastating than having their house of worship destroyed. They could no longer go before the Lord to offer sacrifices for the forgiveness of their sins. But the truth is that their unrepentant sin had already separated them from God (see also Romans 1:18–32). The destruction of the temple was merely the physical manifestation of a spiritual reality.

God explicitly referred to Nebuchadnezzar as His servant and could have raised up any ruler to overtake Judah and Jerusalem, yet the king of Babylon was arrogant and prideful, believing that he'd achieved his power and prestige on his own.

One night, Nebuchadnezzar had a dream, and he summoned Daniel, the wise and faithful prophet of the Lord. God had given Daniel—known in Babylon as Belteshazzar—the gift of interpreting dreams, much like Joseph, who'd interpreted Pharaoh's dreams during the time of the patriarchs.

Daniel not only interpreted the dream but also issued a stern warning for the king: If he didn't give glory to God for his strength and greatness, then "they shall drive you from men, your dwelling shall be with the beasts of the field, and they shall make you eat grass like oxen. They shall wet you with the dew of heaven, and seven times shall pass over you, till you know that the Most High rules in the kingdom of men, and gives it to whomever He chooses.... Therefore, O king, let my advice be acceptable to you; break off your sins by being righteous, and your iniquities by showing mercy to the poor. Perhaps there may be a lengthening of your prosperity" (Daniel 4:25, 27).

Just as the Lord had been patient in not punishing Judah, he gave Nebuchadnezzar a year to repent. Twelve months later, the king was strolling around his palace and said, "Is not this great Babylon, that I have built for a royal dwelling by my mighty power and for the honor of my majesty?" (Daniel 4:30).

We're told that while the words were coming out of his mouth, a voice from heaven spoke, reminding him of the prophecy, and "that very hour the word was fulfilled concerning Nebuchadnezzar" (Daniel 4:33).

Everything Nebuchadnezzar had, from his palace and kingdom to the hair on his head and the breath in his lungs, was his solely because of the Lord's grace and mercy. His refusal to acknowledge this led to him being driven into the wilderness.

Yet the Lord was even there, waiting.

We're never told how long the king dwelled in the wilderness, but one day, he lifted his eyes to heaven, and he blessed, honored, and praised the Most High, speaking the confession in today's verses from Daniel 4:34–35.

In one of the Apostle Peter's Epistles, he admonished the believers: "Therefore humble yourselves under the mighty hand of God, that He may exalt you in due time" (1 Peter 5:6). This is guidance Nebuchadnezzar needed to hear and heed—and it's the same thing our leaders need to hear today. We need to hear it too.

We might look at our leaders and think they're beyond hope. But if the Lord can move the heart of a powerful, prideful, pagan king like Nebuchadnezzar, then no one is beyond His reach.

Let us always remember that "with the Lord one day is as a thousand years, and a thousand years as one day. The Lord is not slack concerning His promise, as some count slackness, but is longsuffering toward us, not willing that any should perish but that all should come to repentance" (2 Peter 3:8–9). And let us pray for humble, repentant leaders who lift their eyes to heaven and praise God.

Prayer

Lord of all creation, as we look at rulers like Nebuchadnezzar or our leaders today, it can be easy to judge them as being prideful and arrogant, deserving of any punishment they receive. However, we're all sinful and fall short of Your glory (Romans 3:23–25). May we all be granted repentant hearts that seek Your face, that You may be glorified, and all whom You've called may be saved. Amen.

For Further Reflection

- In any area of your life, do you feel that the Lord has been "longsuffering" with you? If the situation was in the past, how was God faithful to you during that season? If it's in the present, what would it look like for you to lift your eyes to heaven and repent?
- Have you ever prayed for your governmental authorities by name? If not, give it a try. You can make a list of local, state, and federal officials (councilmen, mayors, sheriffs, district attorneys, governors, congressmen, senators, the president, and so forth), committing to pray for them during their time of service to you, your community, and the nation.

God's Design for Marriage and Family

And the Lord God said, "It is not good that man should be alone;
I will make him a helper comparable to him."...
And the Lord God caused a deep sleep to fall on Adam,
and he slept; and He took one of his ribs, and closed up the flesh
in its place. Then the rib which the Lord God had taken from man
He made into a woman, and He brought her to the man.
And Adam said:
"This is now bone of my bones
And flesh of my flesh;
She shall be called Woman,
Because she was taken out of Man."
Therefore a man shall leave his father and mother
and be joined to his wife, and they shall become one flesh.

—GENESIS 2:18, 21–24

In today's news media, stories abound about how our society is experiencing a "loneliness epidemic." Even though technology has allowed human beings to be more digitally connected than ever before, the sad reality is that these superficial relationships don't fulfill our need for deep, meaningful interactions with other people.

This need for flesh and blood community—especially in marriage and family—is a God-given desire.

After the Lord created Adam, He brought all the animals to him to be named, "but for Adam there was not found a helper comparable to him" (Genesis 2:20). The Lord knew that Adam's solitude was "not good," in contrast to all of creation, which He'd proclaimed "very good" (Genesis 1:31). Unlike the animals, man had no possibility to procreate because he didn't have a suitable counterpart.

Whereas God had created Adam "of the dust of the ground," He created woman by removing the man's rib and forming her from it. The Lord then presented the woman to Adam, who immediately recognized her as his counterpart (Genesis 2:7, 21–23).

You might hear people say that marriage was an invention of the church or the state. Other times you might hear people say things like, "Marriage isn't important—all that matters is that two (or more) people love and respect each other."

All of these and any similar ideas reject the truth we find in Genesis: that God created man, then woman, and that He made them to be one flesh as husband and wife. God Himself instituted marriage—He was the Father who gave away the bride at the wedding and blessed the union. Marriage is a profound mystery, and it is God's intention for this union to provide intimate companionship and mutual support.

However, the highest and foremost purpose of marriage was clearly stated in the command and benediction the Lord spoke to Adam and Eve in Genesis 1:28: "Be fruitful and multiply; fill the earth and subdue it; have dominion over the fish of the sea, over the birds of the air, and over every living thing that moves on the earth." Marriage was and is intended for procreation—for man and woman as one flesh to have children and fill the earth. When children are raised with God's guidance and love from both a mother and a father, they have the opportunity to witness a Christ-centered marriage, receive care and encouragement from both parents, and most important, learn to love the Lord and His Word.

In our fallen world, some marriages don't result in children, through no fault of the husband or wife. Yet that doesn't alter God's original intention for such unions.

The Bible clearly outlines the roles men and women have in marriage. In Ephesians 5:22–24, Paul distinguishes these roles, beginning with wives: "Wives, submit to your own husbands, as to the Lord. For the husband is head of the wife, as also Christ is head of the church; and He is the Savior of the body. Therefore, just as the church is subject to Christ, so let the wives be to their own husbands in everything." And in Colossians 3:18 he writes, "Wives, submit to your own husbands, as is fitting in the Lord."

Today, when people—especially women—hear the word "submit," it's likely to elicit an emotional and rebellious response. After the fall into sin, Eve was burdened with pain in childbirth, but she also was susceptible to resisting her husband's authority: "Your desire shall be for your husband, and he shall rule over you" (Genesis 3:16). While the fall into sin didn't alter God's order of creation, sin did affect marriage dynamics, tainting both Adam's perfect headship and Eve's perfect submission.

Satan's goal is always to drive a wedge between those whom the Lord has joined together, whether husband and wife or parents and children.

Nevertheless, for Christian women, submission is a joy because it's aligned with God's will for them.

Paul also wrote, "Husbands, love your wives and do not be bitter toward them" and "Husbands, love your wives, just as Christ also loved the church and gave Himself for her.... So husbands ought to love their own wives as their own bodies; he who loves his wife loves himself. For no one ever hated his own flesh, but nourishes and cherishes it, just as the Lord does the church" (Colossians 3:19; Ephesians 5:25, 28–29). These verses speak to another purpose of marriage: to reflect the relationship between Christ and His church.

Just as Christ died for His church, a husband should be willing to die for his wife. People in positions of authority, including husbands, are to take the posture of a servant, as Jesus Himself did: "For even the Son of Man did not come to be served, but to serve, and to give His life a ransom for many" (Mark 10:45). When a husband loves his wife in this manner, her submission flows from a place of love and gratitude.

Paul also addressed families in general: "Children, obey your parents in all things, for this is well pleasing to the Lord. Fathers, do not provoke your children, lest they become discouraged" (Colossians 3:20–21). His words in Ephesians 6:1–4 expand on these ideas: "Children, obey your parents in the Lord, for this is right. 'Honor your father and mother,' which is the first commandment with promise: 'that it may be well with you and you may live long on the earth.' And you, fathers, do not provoke your children to wrath, but bring them up in the training and admonition of the Lord."

The parent-child relationship is another area where properly maintaining God's divine design—with parents exercising authority over their children and children submitting to their parents—allows families and individuals to flourish.

God designed marriage as a sacred institution. Marriage and families are the basic building blocks of any thriving nation, and a society that shuns either of these won't succeed.

All we need to do is look at the United States to know that when marriage and families aren't a priority, chaos abounds. We see this in our country's high divorce rate, increased cohabitation apart from marriage, the growing trend of having children out of wedlock and with multiple partners, and ongoing abortion access, among other vices.

Marriage and the traditional family structure have come under significant attack in recent years, and movements to eradicate differences between the sexes—an impossible and foolhardy goal—strive to undermine God's good and holy order of creation. In the same way that shifting tectonic plates cause earthquakes that destroy infrastructure, shifting away from God's design causes tremors that result in societal collapse.

While our current cultural climate might seem dire, we can strive to turn the tide by setting an example for others. In our marriages, wives can submit to husbands, and husbands can love their wives as Christ loved the church. In our families, we can raise our children to fear, love, and obey the Lord. In our communities and nation, we can support laws and organizations that advocate for biblical marriage and families.

Most critical of all, we can share the truth of God's created order with others, as well as the redemption we have in Christ Jesus.

Prayer

Father, when You created Adam and Eve, You established both marriage and the family as the basis for civilization. However, we confess that we haven't done enough to honor Your divine order. In our nation, may You bring about a revitalization of respect for the sanctity of marriage and family, that all might be blessed by the love, peace, and stability that abound when we adhere to Your design. Amen.

For Further Reflection

- In what ways do you think the lack of respect for the institution of marriage has affected our nation?
- How has the breakdown of the biblical family structure impacted individuals, communities, and our nation?

___

___

___

___

___

___

___

The Heart of the Matter

"Now, therefore," says the Lord,
"Turn to Me with all your heart,
With fasting, with weeping, and with mourning."
So rend your heart, and not your garments;
Return to the Lord your God,
For He is gracious and merciful,
Slow to anger, and of great kindness;
And He relents from doing harm.
Who knows if He will turn and relent,
And leave a blessing behind Him—
A grain offering and a drink offering
For the Lord your God?

—JOEL 2:12–14

The kingdom of Judah was struggling. God had sent many prophets, including Joel, to warn His people and call them to repentance, but they refused to listen. Amid their stubborn rebellion, Joel prophesized that the Lord would send His "army," a plague of locusts, to execute His judgment on His people.

Ancient Israelites would have recognized this as God's judgment—one that He'd also inflicted upon Egypt when Pharaoh refused to let God's people worship in the desert, as described in Exodus 10:14–15: "And the locusts went up over all the land of Egypt and rested on all the territory of Egypt. They were very severe; previously there had been no such locusts as they, nor shall there be such after them. For they covered the face of the whole earth, so that the land was darkened; and they ate every herb of the land and all the fruit of the trees which the hail had left. So there remained nothing green on the trees or on the plants of the field throughout all the land of Egypt."

The locust plague would completely wipe out the Israelites' crops, described in vivid detail in Joel 2:3: "A fire devours before them, and behind them a flame burns. The land is like the Garden of Eden before them, and behind them a desolate wilderness; surely nothing shall escape them."

Such complete and utter decimation would lead not only to economic strife but also to physical strife. People would be hungry, and some would starve to death.

Because many of us no longer live or work on farms, and we don't necessarily rely on the successful harvest of a personal crop to feed our families, it can be hard for us to understand the devastation of such an event. While food scarcity is a reality for some in the United States, the majority of Americans are blessed in not having to worry about where their next meal is coming from.

But as devastating as the locust plague and subsequent starvation was, something even more deadly had stricken the land: a famine of faith.

Since the nation of Israel had divided into north and south, Judah had been declining. Devout kings and prophets had helped reignite the people's faith and faithfulness on occasion, but those revivals never lasted. So it was that Judah—the very tribe God had selected as the one from which the Messiah would come—had forsaken the Lord. Forsaken His word and His law. Forsaken worship.

Do you ever feel like the United States has been decimated by a figurative locust plague? That we, too, have lost our way as a nation? That we've forsaken the Lord, His word, His law, and true worship?

We might wish this weren't the case, but year after year, it seems that fewer Americans identify as Christians, let alone as regular church attendees or Bible readers.

Throughout the Old Testament, we see numerous instances of when God allowed tragedy—whether "natural" disasters like the locust plague or an invasion by a foreign army—as a way to draw His people back to Him. If only we weren't so stiff-necked that such methods are sometimes needed!

Yet in His love, the Lord sent prophet after prophet to call His people to repentance. Joel was just one of these faithful messengers who spoke God's truth even at the risk of their lives. As far as earthly esteem and reward were concerned, being a prophet of the Lord was a thankless calling.

In Joel 2:12, the prophet delivers words directly from the mouth of God, admonishing the people to fast, weep, and mourn. When was the last time you considered fasting from food, drink, the internet, news media, or anything else that draws you away from God? Have you ever teared up at the state of our nation, at the horrific things that happen each and every day within our borders? Do ongoing tragedies like legalized abortion cause you to mourn?

Although the Lord commands fasting, weeping, and mourning, these acts are meant to be an outward demonstration of His true concern: the hearts of His people.

The Lord Himself tells His people to "turn to Me with all your heart" (Joel 2:12), which might remind us of what Jesus says is the "first and greatest commandment": "You shall love the Lord your God with all your heart, with all your soul, and with all your mind" (Matthew 22:37–38).

Joel tells the people to rend their hearts and not their garments. It's easy enough to playact repentance, donning sackcloth and dumping ashes on one's head, but the Lord knows what's in every person's heart. He seeks true repentance from each and every sinner—that is, each and every one of us.

So what happens when you rend your heart? Or when a nation rends its heart? It returns to the Lord—and He then relents from doing harm (Jeremiah 18:7–10).

As a nation, let us turn to the One True God, who is indeed "gracious and merciful, slow to anger, and of great kindness"!

Prayer

Lord of all creation, we confess that, like the nation of Judah, we have turned away from You. Yet You are "slow to anger, and of great kindness," showing us mercy in spite of our transgressions (Joel 2:13). May we rend our hearts and return to You—as individuals, as a church, and as a country. In Jesus's name we pray. Amen.

For Further Reflection

- What are some of the "locust plagues" that have afflicted America?
- How can the church set an example of what it looks like to "return to the Lord"? How can you set such an example?

Now into Your heart we pour
Prayers that from our hearts proceeded.
Our petitions heav'nward soar;
May our hearts' desires be heeded!
Write the name we now have given;
Write it in the book of heaven!

"Dearest Jesus, We Are Here"

The Call to Purity

You have heard that it was said to those of old,
"You shall not commit adultery." But I say to you that
whoever looks at a woman to lust for her has already
committed adultery with her in his heart.

—MATTHEW 5:27–28

American culture is saturated with sexual immorality, leaving it in complete discord with God's teachings. This failure to keep His law has led to serious issues, including pornography, rampant adultery, abortion, increased rates of divorce, pedophilia, and an acceptance of homosexual relationships. Every one of these problems has a devastating effect not only on individuals but also on families, communities, and the nation.

In Genesis 1:28, God gave Adam and Eve the blessing and command to "be fruitful and multiply." While sex within the confines of marriage is meant to be pleasurable, it's also meant for a specific purpose: procreation. Any sexual activity outside the confines of that one-flesh union corrupts what God intended for good.

The Ten Commandments specifically address sexual behavior: "You shall not commit adultery" and "You shall not covet your neighbor's house; you shall not covet your neighbor's wife, nor his male servant, nor his female servant, nor his ox, nor his donkey, nor anything that is your neighbor's" (Exodus 20:14, 17). The penalty for having sexual relations outside of marriage was death: "The man who commits adultery with another man's wife, he who commits adultery with his neighbor's wife, the adulterer and the adulteress, shall surely be put to death" (Leviticus 20:10).

Though this punishment might seem extreme to modern sensibilities, the reason is provided in a more detailed listing of laws related to sexual morality found in Deuteronomy 22:22: "If a man is found lying with a woman married to a husband, then both of them shall die—the man that lay with the woman, and the woman; *so you shall put away the evil from Israel*" (emphasis added). The Lord is holy, and as His chosen people and representatives on earth, He expected the Israelites to be holy too.

These laws were particularly important in the larger context of the world the Israelites inhabited, because many of the surrounding nations worshipped false gods with rituals that involved sexual activity. Thus, it's no coincidence that when Israel went astray, their rebellion was portrayed as adultery: "I will not have mercy on her children, for they are the children of harlotry. For their mother has played the harlot; she who conceived them has behaved shamefully. For she said, 'I will go after my lovers, who give me my bread and my water, my wool and my linen, my oil and my drink'" (Hosea 2:4–5).

The adultery metaphor was used throughout the Old Testament to warn the people to return to the Lord. If they did so, the Lord painted a picture of reconciliation: "I will betroth you to Me forever; yes, I will betroth you to Me in righteousness and justice, in lovingkindness and mercy; I will betroth you to Me in faithfulness, and you shall know the Lord" (Hosea 2:19–20). This prophecy was fulfilled through the life, death, and resurrection of Jesus Christ: "Now all things are of God, who has reconciled us to Himself through Jesus Christ, and has given us the ministry of reconciliation, that is, that God was in Christ reconciling the world to Himself, not imputing their trespasses to them, and has committed to us the word of reconciliation" (2 Corinthians 5:18–19).

The church is often referred to as the bride of Christ, and we read a beautiful picture of this union in Revelation: "'Let us be glad and rejoice and give Him glory, for the marriage of the Lamb has come, and His wife has made herself ready.' And to her it was granted to be arrayed in fine linen, clean and bright, for the fine linen is the righteous acts of the saints" (Revelation 19:7–8).

Paul merges these ideas in his first letter to the Corinthians, telling the congregation, "Do you not know that your bodies are members of Christ? Shall I then take the members of Christ and make them members of a harlot? Certainly not! Or do you not know that he who is joined to a harlot is one body with her? For 'the two,' He says, 'shall become one flesh.' But he who is joined to the Lord is one spirit with Him. Flee sexual immorality. Every sin that a man does is outside the body, but he who commits sexual immorality sins against his own body" (1 Corinthians 6:15–18).

This passage highlights the sanctity of the body and the serious nature of sexual sin. When we commit sexual sin, we not only violate the unity of flesh intended for marriage alone but also contaminate our fellowship with God. Each act that goes against God's intended purpose for sex—whether seducing, looking lustfully at someone who isn't your spouse, viewing sexual content, or fornicating—defiles us and distances us from the holiness we're called to in Christ, "for all that is in the world—the lust of the flesh, the lust of the eyes, and the pride of life—is not of the Father but is of the world" (1 John 2:16).

Jeremiah 17:9 proclaims, "The heart is deceitful above all things, and desperately wicked; who can know it?" Jesus identified the heart as the source of all sin, including sexual immorality: "What comes out of a man, that defiles a man. For from within, out of the heart of men, proceed evil thoughts, adulteries, fornications, murders, thefts, covetousness, wickedness, deceit, lewdness, an evil eye, blasphemy, pride, foolishness. All these evil things come from within and defile a man" (Mark 7:20–23). Only by God's grace can we overcome our fleshly desires, empowered by His Holy Spirit.

In Christ we find redemption for all of our sins, including sexual immorality. When the scribes and Pharisees brought to Jesus a woman caught in adultery, He said, "He who is without sin among you, let him throw a stone at her first" (John 8:7). Gradually, each of her accusers left, and she stood alone with Jesus. He asked her, "Woman, where are those accusers of yours? Has no one condemned you?" (John 8:10). To which she replied, "No one, Lord." And He told her, "Neither do I condemn you; go and sin no more" (John 8:11).

The United States desperately needs a return to a biblical understanding of marriage and sexuality, as well as to the virtues of modesty, purity, and chastity. May we Christians lead the charge in promoting God's design for one man and one woman in marriage, and raise our children to honor it as well. And may all who have committed sexual immorality repent, seeking forgiveness and restoration in Jesus Christ.

Prayer

Heavenly Father, we come before You acknowledging that our nation falls far short of Your standards for sexual purity—and so do we. Help us to resist temptation and pursue purity in thought, word, and deed, and let us strive to promote biblical values about sexuality in our families and communities. Thank You for reminding us that in Christ, we are forgiven and called out of darkness into His glorious light. In His name we pray. Amen.

For Further Reflection

- In what ways has a movement away from biblical concepts of marriage and sexuality led to the social ills we see today?
- How can the church and individual believers help those who are caught up in sexual sin?

____

____

____

____

____

____

Being Subject to Rulers and Authorities

Remind them to be subject to rulers and authorities, to obey, to be ready for every good work, to speak evil of no one, to be peaceable, gentle, showing all humility to all men.

—TITUS 3:1–2

Ever since Adam and Eve disobeyed God in the Garden of Eden, mankind has resisted authority—*all* authority. We rebel against our parents. We cheat on tests in school. We lie to our bosses. We break laws. (Be honest: Do you always drive the speed limit? You'd be hard-pressed to find someone who does!)

And just like our first parents, we disobey our Heavenly Father.

Considering our rebellious, sinful nature, it's no surprise that in Paul's letter to Titus, he instructs the young pastor to encourage his flock "to be subject to rulers and authorities."

At this point in history, Crete was part of the massive Roman Empire. Like many locations along the Mediterranean Sea, this large island was a bustling hub of commerce and multiculturalism. People from all nations, creeds, and religions lived in and traveled through Crete, including the capital city of Gortyn, situated in the island's southern region. Gortyn had long been famous in Greek culture, and it's even mentioned in the works of both Homer and Plato, two of Greece's most famous writers.

The Cretan church was founded in Gortyn, and Titus, one of Paul's children in the faith, served as its first bishop.

Similar to other places where churches were established in the first century, friction existed between Christianity and Judaism. Jewish leaders resented and tried to squelch this new "sect" based on the teachings of Jesus Christ, whom they perceived to be nothing more than a blasphemous preacher and a false messiah. We're told in the book of Acts, and in some of Paul's Epistles, that before his conversion, he himself was persecuting Christians: "As for Saul [Paul], he made havoc of the church, entering every house, and dragging off men and women, committing them to prison" (Acts 8:3).

Christians also faced persecution from those who practiced false religions, such as worship of the Roman gods and emperor.

These realities are highlighted throughout Acts, as Paul repeatedly faced rejection and abuse from many Jews, as well as antagonism and threats of execution from the Roman authorities—threats they'd eventually fulfill when they martyred him in Rome.

When we read about the sufferings of first-century Christians, we might think we don't have anything in common with those early believers and the world they inhabited. After all, we live in a completely different time and place—a modern, more civilized era. Our lives aren't at stake simply for saying the name "Jesus Christ."

Indeed, we're blessed to live in a nation where we can freely proclaim our faith and worship the One True God. Yet our brothers and sisters in Christ across the globe face the same kinds of persecutions Paul and other first-century Christians faced.

But we should never become complacent, thinking, *Oh, that would never happen here.*

As our nation becomes increasingly pagan, tensions between the culture and the church will surely increase. We've already seen situations where Christians have been taken to court because they refused to provide services that went against their beliefs. And churches were fined for refusing to close their doors during a health scare. These are merely two examples of this tension.

While we might not be compelled to worship our civil leaders as gods, we're certainly encouraged to trust and rely on them for all our needs—instead of trusting and relying on God alone for all things. And though at present we might not be persecuted in the same ways the early church was, we often experience the friction of being Christians in a country that has been drifting away from the Lord and His law.

The Cretan Christians were reminded to obey a government that could be openly hostile to them and their faith. And Paul's admonishment "to be subject to rulers and authorities" applies to us even today. Though we "ought to obey God rather than men" (Acts 5:29), as long as our government or any other authority is asking us to do something that neither violates God's law nor goes against Christian conscience, we're to submit to them—even if we disagree with their policies or decisions.

It's important to keep in mind that how we relate to our Lord's appointed authorities reflects our obedience to Him and our witness to the world. When we trust and rely on the Lord for all things, it's easy to obey earthly authorities because we know that He is ultimately in control, not them.

How do we deal with any tension between the church and our culture or government? The same way Paul instructed Titus to teach his congregation: do good works, speak no evil, and be peaceable, gentle, and humble. In short, imitate our Lord and Savior Jesus Christ in all we say and do (Ephesians 5:1–2).

What this might look like in practice is to positively contribute to society: honor our spouse, raise our children to love and fear God, be a law-abiding citizen, volunteer for our church and community organizations, and be a source of encouragement, as well as God-led censure, to all leaders God has placed in a position of authority over us.

The grace and forgiveness we've received from our Savior should compel us to love and serve our neighbor, as He instructs us: "Let your light so shine before men, that they may see your good works and glorify your Father in heaven" (Matthew 5:16).

Prayer

Lord of glory, You are the ultimate ruler and authority of all things, both visible and invisible. Yet we often rebel against You. May we repent of the times we've sinned against You and the authorities You've placed over us. In the name of Your Son Jesus Christ. Amen.

For Further Reflection

- In what ways do you see a lack of people being "subject to rulers and authorities" in the United States? How does this affect our country?
- How do you rebel against God-appointed authority in your own life? How does that affect you and your relationships?

Doing What Is Good, Right, and True

Thus Hezekiah did throughout all Judah, and he did what was good and right and true before the Lord his God. And in every work that he began in the service of the house of God, in the law and in the commandment, to seek his God, he did it with all his heart. So he prospered.

—2 CHRONICLES 31:20–21

Have you ever seen or heard a leader who was truly inspiring? Someone who made you think things like *I'd follow that person anywhere*, or *That's the kind of leader I want to be*?

In ancient Israel, King Hezekiah of Judah was that kind of leader.

So, what can we learn from him about the kind of leaders we should be, as well as the kind of leaders we want for our country?

When Hezekiah first ascended the throne, Judah was in a deep state of apostasy that had taken root under the previous king, Ahaz: "For the Lord brought Judah low because of Ahaz king of Israel, for he had encouraged moral decline in Judah and had been continually unfaithful to the Lord" (2 Chronicles 28:19). It was bad enough that Ahaz was idolatrous, but he sinned all the more in leading many astray.

The people's transgressions were so extreme that God brought judgment upon Ahaz: "Therefore the Lord his God delivered him into the hand of the king of Syria. They defeated him, and carried away a great multitude of them as captives, and brought them to Damascus. Then he was also delivered into the hand of the king of Israel, who defeated him with a great slaughter" (2 Chronicles 28:5).

Instead of this judgment bringing about repentance, it seemed that the king dug in his heels: "Now in the time of his distress King Ahaz became increasingly unfaithful to the Lord. This is that King Ahaz. For he sacrificed to the gods of Damascus which had defeated him, saying, 'Because the gods of the kings of Syria help them, I will sacrifice to them that they may help me.' But they were the ruin of him and of all Israel" (2 Chronicles 28:22–23).

When he was afraid and unsure of what to do, Ahaz squandered an opportunity to throw himself on the Lord's mercy, to seek forgiveness and ask for wisdom and protection for both himself and his subjects. But he doubled down on his idolatry, and the nation suffered.

Throughout the books detailing the respective rulers of Judah and Israel, the good kings are often described as Hezekiah was: "He did what was right in the sight of the Lord, according to all that his father David had done" (2 Chronicles 29:2). In the Bible, David is the gold standard of kings, described as "a man after [God's] own heart" because of his zeal for, trust in, and obedience to the Lord (1 Samuel 13:14; see also Acts 13:22).

Hezekiah was only twenty-five years old when he became king, and from a worldly perspective, his accomplishments were all the more astounding in view of his youth. But the key to his success was his dedication not only to being a wise and just ruler but also to living a life aligned with God's will, doing "what was good and right and true before the Lord his God" (2 Chronicles 31:20).

Within the first month of his reign, Hezekiah didn't waste any time in establishing his top priority as king, and "he opened the doors of the house of the Lord and repaired them. Then he brought in the priests and the Levites, and gathered them in the East Square" (2 Chronicles 29:3–4). He reopened the temple and rallied the preachers and teachers of the Law, recommissioning them and ordering them to sanctify the temple, the worship articles, and themselves, so that worship of the Lord could be restored, and His holy wrath might subside.

After the temple was set back in order, "King Hezekiah rose early, gathered the rulers of the city, and went up to the house of the Lord" (2 Chronicles 29:20). The king understood that to ensure the people returned to God, the leaders needed to have a united front. They needed to set an example for the people by bringing their sin offerings to the temple and properly worshipping the Lord. The king then invited the people to bring their sacrifices.

Hezekiah recognized that their most important priority as a nation was to worship God in purity and truth. In addition to reinstituting temple worship, he kept the Passover for the first time in many years. But this wasn't limited to Judah; he also invited the northern tribes to celebrate the feast. Extending this olive branch to their estranged brethren—giving them an opportunity to fellowship with the Lord and recall all the wonders He'd done for their forefathers—was a gracious act. When the invitations went out, "the hand of God was on Judah to give them singleness of heart to obey the command of the king and the leaders, at the word of the Lord" (2 Chronicles 30:12).

The people answered Hezekiah's summons in droves, and the description of their celebration is a beautiful picture of what it looks like to be in fellowship with the Lord and other believers: "So there was great joy in Jerusalem, for since the time of Solomon the son of David, king of Israel, there had been nothing like this in Jerusalem. Then the priests, the Levites, arose and blessed the people, and their voice was heard; and their prayer came up to His holy dwelling place, to heaven" (2 Chronicles 30:26–27). In the years since Solomon ruled, the people had fallen in and out of faithfulness to God. But in this extraordinary moment, their praise and prayers ascended to the very throne of the Most High.

When Sennacherib, king of Assyria, sought to overthrow Judah, Hezekiah encouraged his military leaders and told them that they needn't fear because "with him is an arm of flesh; but with us is the Lord our God, to help us and to fight our battles" (2 Chronicles 32:8). The king trusted that as long as the Lord was on their side, the prophet Isaiah's words would hold true: "No weapon formed against you shall prosper" (Isaiah 54:17).

In another profound scene, when Sennacherib and his servants sought to overthrow Judah, they blasphemed against the Lord: "King Hezekiah and the prophet Isaiah, the son of Amoz, prayed and cried out to heaven. Then the Lord sent an angel who cut down every mighty man of valor, leader, and captain in the camp of the king of Assyria" (2 Chronicles 32:20–21). We find even more information about this event in 2 Kings 19, which tells us that anytime these enemies challenged Hezekiah, he "went up to the house of the Lord" (2 Kings 19:14). He stood before the Lord and prayed powerful intercessory prayers on behalf of his nation. And the Lord honored these prayers, telling the king through Isaiah, "Thus says the Lord God of Israel: 'Because you have prayed to Me against Sennacherib king of Assyria, I have heard'" (2 Kings 19:20).

When we reflect on Hezekiah's reign, we can see that his success stemmed not from might and riches but from adopting a posture of humility and complete dependence on God. America needs leaders who embody this same spirit—who actively seek wisdom and guidance from the Lord and pray not for their personal ambitions and aspirations but for the welfare of the entire nation. We can pray for God to raise up leaders like Hezekiah, who understand that true greatness doesn't come from power and wealth but from a heart that's aligned with God's will in Christ Jesus.

Prayer

Dear Lord, Your servant Hezekiah led a great revival in the nation of Judah, shepherding his subjects back to true worship of You. May You bless our nation with leaders who seek You first in all circumstances and in every decision, having true hearts of public servants who put others' needs before their own. May this be done according to Your holy and perfect will. Amen.

For Further Reflection

- How do you think our local, state, and federal governments would function if worshipping the Lord was the priority, and our leaders sought His guidance and prayed for His intercession?
- The next time you receive or read distressing news, how could you take that concern before the Lord, praying an intercessory prayer on behalf of those affected?

Stewardship of the Land

For the earnest expectation of the creation eagerly waits for the revealing of the sons of God. For the creation was subjected to futility, not willingly, but because of Him who subjected it in hope; because the creation itself also will be delivered from the bondage of corruption into the glorious liberty of the children of God. For we know that the whole creation groans and labors with birth pangs together until now.

—ROMANS 8:19–22

Once in a while, I ponder how much fun God must have had during the six days of creation.

How did He decide what color everything would be? How did He come up with the idea for our solar system and each of the unique and fascinating planets? What's the deal with the platypus?

All these questions and more race through my head every time I read the first two chapters of Genesis.

For six days, the Lord created everything we see around us in nature, and at the very end, He "saw everything that He had made, and indeed it was very good" (Genesis 1:31). God placed Adam "in the garden of Eden to tend and keep it" (Genesis

2:15), and after He created Eve, he positioned the first husband and wife as stewards over all creation, instructing them to "be fruitful and multiply; fill the earth and subdue it; have dominion over the fish of the sea, over the birds of the air, and over every living thing that moves on the earth" (Genesis 1:28).

With our modern sensibilities, the words "subdue" and "dominion" often have negative connotations, eliciting thoughts of oppression and abuse. Yet that wasn't the case in the context of the Lord's flawless creation. Adam and Eve were in harmony with one another and with all that surrounded them. Subduing and having dominion meant nothing more than obeying God by exercising the special authority He'd given them over all the earth. And because they hadn't fallen into sin, they'd execute these tasks perfectly.

But after they ate of the tree of the knowledge of good and evil, creation itself was cursed because of their sin: "Cursed is the ground for your sake; in toil you shall eat of it all the days of your life. Both thorns and thistles it shall bring forth for you, and you shall eat the herb of the field" (Genesis 3:17–18). No longer would their easy labor produce a delicious crop. Even when they did backbreaking work in the heat of the sun, there was no guarantee their efforts would produce much of anything.

Paul writes in Romans 8:22, "For we know that the whole creation groans and labors with birth pangs together until now." This statement connects Adam's sin with Eve's sin; she was told by God, "I will greatly multiply your sorrow and your conception; in pain you shall bring forth children" (Genesis 3:16). Now only through hard labor would Adam bring forth food from the ground and Eve children from her body.

The fall into sin reverberated deeply throughout all of creation. The world became broken, full of decay and death. Frustrated nature stands as a reminder of mankind's rebellion against God and the corruption and disharmony that ensued because of our disobedience.

In spite of its flawed and fallen state, God still loves His creation, and we find this truth throughout the Bible. One of the clearest pieces of evidence can be found in His instructions in the Mosaic law: "Speak to the children of Israel, and say to them: 'When you come into the land which I give you, then the land shall keep a sabbath to the Lord. Six years you shall sow your field, and six years you shall prune your vineyard, and gather its fruit; but in the seventh year there shall be a sabbath of solemn rest for the land, a sabbath to the Lord. You shall neither sow your field nor prune your vineyard'" (Leviticus 25:2–4).

God loved the land so much that He didn't want His people to destroy it by overworking it. The Sabbath rest would give it an opportunity to regenerate. Additionally, the Israelites could demonstrate their trust in Him, that even if they left the land fallow, they'd still have enough food to feed their families and their servants, and their livestock.

This law also served to remind the Israelites that the land wasn't theirs—it was the Lord's. Psalm 44:2–3 says, "You drove out the nations with Your hand, but them You planted; You afflicted the peoples, and cast them out. For they did not gain possession of the land by their own sword, nor did their own arm save them; but it was Your right hand, Your arm, and the light of Your countenance, because You favored them."

The Lord always keeps His word, so when the Israelites disobeyed the command in Leviticus 25:2–4—along with every other command He'd given through Moses—they were punished by King Nebuchadnezzar, who took the kingdom of Judah into captivity: "And those who escaped from the sword he carried away to Babylon, where they became servants to him and his sons until the rule of the kingdom of Persia, to fulfill the word of the Lord by the mouth of Jeremiah, until the land had enjoyed her Sabbaths. As long as she lay desolate she kept Sabbath, to fulfill seventy years" (2 Chronicles 36:20–21).

The way the Israelites chose to steward the land they'd been given communicated something about their trust in God—just as the way we choose to steward our land and its resources communicates our beliefs about the One who created them.

Psalm 104:14 says, "He causes the grass to grow for the cattle, and vegetation for the service of man, that he may bring forth food from the earth." Although human beings work the ground, it's ultimately the Lord who commands His creation. It serves purposes designed by Him, which we should strive to preserve.

In the New Testament, we see God's mastery over creation when Jesus performs His miracles. Whether turning water into wine, calming a storm, walking on water, or healing the lame or blind, each act demonstrates that He can use His power to love His creation and glorify the Father.

These days, there's a heightened concern among many about the environment. On the one hand, there are groups who insist that the earth will meet an untimely demise if we don't perform certain actions, whether as individuals or as nations. On the other hand, there are those who misuse God's command to subdue the earth and have dominion over it as a license for destruction. Both perspectives are prideful attitudes that discredit the biblical truth that creation isn't ours to save or destroy: the Lord will sustain this world until He deems it's time for it to pass away. At that point, creation will finally be "delivered from the bondage of corruption," when Jesus Christ returns to make all things new (Romans 8:21).

Until then, let us trust the Lord "in whose hand is the life of every living thing, and the breath of all mankind" (Job 12:10), demonstrating our reverence to Him through proper stewardship and humbly recognizing that we are privileged caretakers of His marvelous creation.

Prayer

Lord, Psalm 24:1 says, "The earth is [Yours], and all its fullness." As we gaze in wonder at the beauty of Your creation all around us, may it humble us to remember that You rule over and are in control of all things, in heaven and on earth. Please help us, individually and as a nation, to be good stewards of the earth, that we may honor the work of Your hands and bring glory to Your holy name. Amen.

For Further Reflection

- The term "eco-anxiety" reflects a fear that human activities will irreparably harm our earth. What do you think is the source of this fear?
- Do you think that our nation's approach to environmental matters reflects proper stewardship of God's creation? Why or why not?

O come, Desire of nations, bind
In one the hearts of all mankind;
Bid thou our sad divisions cease,
And be Thyself our King of Peace.
Rejoice! Rejoice!
Emmanuel Shall come to thee, O Israel!

"O Come, O Come, Emmanuel"

For the Lord's Sake

Therefore submit yourselves to every ordinance of man for the Lord's sake, whether to the king as supreme, or to governors, as to those who are sent by him for the punishment of evildoers and for the praise of those who do good. For this is the will of God, that by doing good you may put to silence the ignorance of foolish men—as free, yet not using liberty as a cloak for vice, but as bondservants of God. Honor all people. Love the brotherhood. Fear God. Honor the king.

—1 PETER 2:13–17

One hallmark of the United States is that from its inception, it went against the notion of "divine right" that many sovereigns, whether just or unjust, used as validation for their rule. The Declaration of Independence eloquently asserted the truth that all men are created equal, and they have certain unalienable rights given to them by their Creator.

Today, we often take for granted the idea of unalienable rights, because we're so accustomed to them and have never lived any other way. If we visited a country that didn't hold these same truths, we'd likely be in for a rude awakening.

When the Apostle Peter wrote his first Epistle, Christianity had been spreading throughout the Roman Empire for about thirty years and was well established in some areas. In spite of its ever-increasing prevalence, the early Christians encountered a lot of resistance to what many considered nothing more than a new sect of Judaism.

Peter was intimately familiar with resisting both civil and religious authorities for the sake of the Gospel. We read about many of these exploits in the first twelve chapters of the book of Acts.

At Pentecost, Peter called the people to repentance and boldly proclaimed the resurrected Christ to the Jews gathered in Jerusalem, and "those who gladly received his word were baptized; and that day about three thousand souls were added to them" (Acts 2:41). Sometime after Pentecost, Peter and John went to the temple. They healed a man who had been born lame, and the people who saw it were amazed (Acts 3:11).

Then Peter preached another powerful sermon of repentance and forgiveness. While he was speaking, "the priests, the captain of the temple, and the Sadducees came upon them, being greatly disturbed that they taught the people and preached in Jesus the resurrection from the dead. And they laid hands on them, and put them in custody" (Acts 4:1–3). As effective as the Pentecost sermon had been, even more people—five thousand men—were converted after this sermon.

The next day, when Peter and John were dragged in front of the Jewish leaders, Peter once again boldly confessed Christ. Since the Jewish leaders couldn't deny the healing miracle that was performed, they "commanded [Peter and John] not to speak at all nor preach in the name of Jesus" (Acts 4:18). Before they were released, Peter replied, "Whether it is right in the sight of God to listen to you more than to God, you judge. For we cannot but speak the things which we have seen and heard" (Acts 4:19–20). Long gone was the Peter who had denied Jesus three times, replaced by a man who stood against the authorities to preach the Gospel.

Later in Acts, King Herod "stretched out his hand to harass some from the church. Then he killed James the brother of John with the sword. And because he saw that it pleased the Jews, he proceeded to seize Peter also.... So when he had arrested him, he put him in prison, and delivered him to four squads of soldiers to keep him, intending to bring him before the people after Passover" (Acts 12:1–4). Although this Herod is not the king who'd ordered the murder of the male children in Bethlehem, he had the same bloodthirsty bent as his forebear.

That night, while Peter was sleeping, the Lord sent an angel to free him, and he escaped. He immediately went to find the brethren and "declared to them how the Lord had brought him out of the prison" (Acts 12:17).

God had more work for Peter to do to further His kingdom, but one day, he'd meet the fate Jesus prophesied in John 21:18–19: "'Most assuredly, I say to you, when you were younger, you girded yourself and walked where you wished; but when you are old, you will stretch out your hands, and another will gird you and carry you where you do not wish.' This He spoke, signifying by what death he would glorify God."

Peter was martyred in AD 68. According to tradition, he was crucified upside down because he didn't feel worthy to die in the same manner as our Savior. He lived out what he preached, being obedient to the civil authorities, even unto death. When the Lord saw fit to allow him to continue preaching the Gospel, he was to be a fisher of men. But when his appointed time of death arrived, he "[rejoiced] that [he was] counted worthy to suffer shame for His name" (Acts 5:41).

We, too, should strive to live out what Peter commands in these verses from his first Epistle. For the Lord's sake, we can submit to the rulers the Lord has placed over us, recognizing that their purpose is to punish those who do evil and reward those who do good—even when the rulers themselves are evil, or we disagree with their decisions or actions.

When we're persecuted, our good works will vouch for us before the civil authorities and any false accusers, "for rulers are not a terror to good works, but to evil" (Romans 13:3). Immediately preceding today's passage, in 1 Peter 2:12, the apostle said we should ensure that our "conduct [is] honorable among the Gentiles, that when they speak against [us] as evildoers, they may, by [our] good works which they observe, glorify God in the day of visitation," thus revealing the ultimate purpose of our works: to bring glory to God and lead people to the knowledge of the truth of the Gospel.

And let us not use our Christian liberty "as a cloak for vice," knowing that we are forgiven (1 Peter 2:16). As Paul wrote in Romans 6:1–2, "Shall we continue in sin that grace may abound? Certainly not!"

We're to honor everyone, love our brothers and sisters in Christ, fear the Lord, and honor the king (1 Peter 2:17). How blessed we are to have examples of believers like the Apostle Peter, as we use our freedom in Christ to serve God and neighbor.

Prayer

Dear Jesus, Your apostle Peter rightly proclaimed, "We ought to obey God rather than men" (Acts 5:29). Thank You for discipling him and molding him into a bold leader with a bold confession of faith, which helped provide a solid foundation for Your church. May we be similarly uncompromising in our commitment to You, clinging fast to Your truth until the very end. Amen.

For Further Reflection

- In your opinion, what are some of the greatest sources of tension between our civil authorities and the church?
- Have you ever been in a situation when you felt it necessary to challenge someone in authority? How did you handle the situation? Should or could you have done anything differently?

____

____

____

____

____

____

____

____

And God Relented

So the people of Nineveh believed God, proclaimed a fast, and put on sackcloth, from the greatest to the least of them. Then word came to the king of Nineveh; and he arose from his throne and laid aside his robe, covered himself with sackcloth and sat in ashes. And he caused it to be proclaimed and published throughout Nineveh by the decree of the king and his nobles, saying, "Let neither man nor beast, herd nor flock, taste anything; do not let them eat, or drink water. But let man and beast be covered with sackcloth, and cry mightily to God; yes, let every one turn from his evil way and from the violence that is in his hands. Who can tell if God will turn and relent, and turn away from His fierce anger, so that we may not perish?" Then God saw their works, that they turned from their evil way; and God relented from the disaster that He had said He would bring upon them, and He did not do it.

—JONAH 3:5–10

If you grew up attending Sunday school, it's highly likely you read the story of Jonah. However, you might not have learned much beyond the fact that he ran away from God and was swallowed by a large fish, in whose belly he stayed for three days.

Yet there's so much more to this story.

After those three days, that portion of the Jonah narrative ends in a fascinating way: "So the Lord spoke to the fish, and it vomited Jonah onto dry land" (Jonah 2:10). The fish was even more obedient to God's command than the prophet had been, immediately doing what it was instructed to do.

Once Jonah was ready to obey the Lord, he prepared to traverse the entire city of Nineveh, which we're told was "an exceedingly great city, a three-day journey in extent" with "more than one hundred and twenty thousand persons" (Jonah 3:3, 4:11). All the while, the prophet declared the Lord's intentions for the city: "Yet forty days, and Nineveh will be overthrown!" (Jonah 3:4).

Just as Jonah was in the fish's belly for three days and was brought back from the dead, for the three days Jonah proclaimed judgment on the Ninevites, they were as good as dead if God didn't relent.

Nineveh was the capital of the Assyrian Empire and renowned for its wickedness. Another minor prophet, Nahum, decried its reputation and deeds: "Woe to the bloody city! It is all full of lies and robbery. Its victim never departs.... There is a multitude of slain, a great number of bodies, countless corpses—they stumble over the corpses—because of the multitude of harlotries of the seductive harlot, the mistress of sorceries, who sell nations through her harlotries, and families through her sorceries" (Nahum 3:1, 3–4). One can understand why our holy Lord would determine to condemn such a place, as its inhabitants were destroying not only people's lives but also their souls. (You can read about a similar situation with Sodom and Gomorrah in Genesis 18–19.)

Jonah's preaching had an instant result. The people fasted and put on sackcloth—and not just some people: *everyone*, "from the greatest to the least of them," and the king himself left his throne and finery to join his people in repentance (Jonah 3:5–6). Even the livestock were enlisted for the cause (Jonah 3:7). Although God didn't ask or tell the Ninevites to fast or don sackcloth, these outward demonstrations reflected the fact that "the people of Nineveh believed God" and that He would destroy them in forty days if they didn't "turn from [their] evil way and from the violence that is in [their] hands" (Jonah 3:5, 8). Centuries later, Jesus Himself would commend their behavior: "The men of Nineveh will rise up in the judgment with this generation and condemn it, for they repented at the preaching of Jonah; and indeed a greater than Jonah is here" (Luke 11:32).

The king and his subjects cried out to God, praying that He'd spare them, and that's exactly what He did: "Then God saw their works, that they turned from their evil way; and God relented from the disaster that He had said He would bring upon them, and He did not do it" (Jonah 3:10).

Such a glorious demonstration of the Lord's grace!

At this point, you might think that Jonah would be happy. After all, his preaching had resulted in God forgiving an entire city of people, and the Lord was glorified. What a humbling honor, right?

Not to Jonah, who was the opposite of happy: "But it displeased Jonah exceedingly, and he became angry" (Jonah 4:1). Why was he so angry? As he told the Lord, "for I know that You are a gracious and merciful God, slow to anger and abundant in lovingkindness, One who relents from doing harm" (Jonah 4:2). Basically, Jonah was angry at God for being Himself. "God is love," and He cannot violate His own character (1 John 4:8).

Instead of rejoicing even "over one sinner who repents," Jonah tells God that he'd rather die than witness the Ninevites' deliverance (Luke 15:7; Jonah 4:3).

We might be inclined to judge Jonah. To think he's being harsh, cruel, melodramatic, or unloving. But ask yourself this: Have you ever looked at a city, region, or another country and thought they were surely too evil to be saved? Have you ever thought that about a person or a group of people?

To my shame, I have. Thus, as much as I'd like to cast aspersions on Jonah for his refusal to preach a gospel of repentance to the Ninevites, I must confess that at times I've been no different. We've all fallen short in this regard, because none of us can perfectly love our neighbors—or God—as we should.

God is "not willing that any should perish but that all should come to repentance" (2 Peter 3:9). As Christians, we should reflect this same mercy. When we observe nations, communities, or individuals who stand against God, we might be inclined to condemn or avoid them. But we must do what Jonah both succeeded and failed to do—rebuke evil yet see ourselves as numbered among the sinners, in desperate need of salvation: "But God demonstrates His own love toward us, in that while we were still sinners, Christ died for us" (Romans 5:8).

Instead of harboring resentment or fear toward those who hate the Lord, we are called to pray for their repentance and salvation. This is indeed a humbling honor, to pray for God's enemies and ours.

Prayer

Lord Almighty, You are slow to anger and abounding in love, steadfast and merciful. You don't punish us as we deserve, for Your Son, Jesus Christ, took our punishment on Himself, dying on the cross for the sins of the whole world. Let us be diligent in sharing His love with others, most especially those who neither know nor fear You, that they may be brought to repentance through the hearing of Your Word. Thank You for this honor. Amen.

For Further Reflection

- Are there any nations, groups of people, or a specific person you find it hard to pray for? If so, what steps can you take to genuinely intercede for them, trusting in God's power to bring people to faith?
- Has there even been a point in your life when you weren't a believer? During this time, was anyone praying for your salvation? If you know anyone who did, reach out to that person and thank them, if you can do so.

____

____

____

____

____

____

____

Guarding Our Hearts and Minds

Be anxious for nothing, but in everything by prayer and supplication, with thanksgiving, let your requests be made known to God; and the peace of God, which surpasses all understanding, will guard your hearts and minds through Christ Jesus.

—PHILIPPIANS 4:6–7

With each passing year, more and more Americans are struggling with anxiety. The causes for this trend are manifold. Spiraling inflation and economic instability raise concerns about affording basic needs. The carnage caused by wars and civil unrest assails our eyes every time we look at the news or social media. Agendas and policies that lead to confusion and chaos abound in every sphere of our society, as even matters of created, immutable biology are disputed. Toxic and divisive politics add stress to our lives, including our interpersonal relationships.

Taking all of this into consideration, it's easy to see why many people are distraught over the state of our nation. Even so, Paul's words in Philippians remind us that Christians can and should respond to distressing current events in a different way.

First, the apostle admonishes us to "be anxious for nothing" (Philippians 4:6). These words echo what Jesus preached in the Sermon on the Mount: "Therefore do not worry, saying, 'What shall we eat?' or 'What shall we drink?' or 'What shall we wear?'... For your heavenly Father knows that you need all these things. But seek first the kingdom of God and His righteousness, and all these things shall be added to you. Therefore do not worry about tomorrow, for tomorrow will worry about its own things. Sufficient for the day is its own trouble" (Matthew 6:31–34).

Jesus tells us that our Heavenly Father is aware of our needs and will provide for them—especially the basic needs to sustain our lives here on earth, like food and clothing. Instead of fretting over these things, Jesus suggests that we seek God's kingdom and righteousness first and foremost, an acknowledgment that while the temporal is important, the eternal is essential. And the more we "set [our] mind[s] on things above," the less we'll be inordinately focused "on things on the earth" (Colossians 3:2).

Next, Paul writes, "But in everything by prayer and supplication, with thanksgiving, let your requests be made known to God" (Philippians 4:6). This is more than a suggestion—it's a command to bring everything that's on our hearts and minds to the Lord. We speak to Him, presenting our petitions and offering thanksgiving for the many ways He has blessed us. Gratitude is an antidote to anxiety, because it reorients our thinking from what-ifs and difficult circumstances toward concrete evidence of God's provision in our lives and His faithfulness to us.

Philippians 4:7 says, "And the peace of God, which surpasses all understanding, will guard your hearts and minds through

Christ Jesus." It's such a comforting, hopeful, and lovely thought, that the peace of God will guard our hearts and minds. But what exactly *is* "the peace of God"? Exploring this word as it's used throughout the life of Jesus can help enhance our understanding, even if the full depth of the meaning is beyond our comprehension.

After Jesus's birth in Bethlehem, an angel announced this event to the shepherds, and "there was with the angel a multitude of the heavenly host praising God and saying: 'Glory to God in the highest, and on earth peace, goodwill toward men!'" (Luke 2:13–14; cf. Luke 19:38). The angels praised the Father and heralded the most critical event in human history. Their proclamation signaled that through this Child, mankind would be reconciled to God, bringing peace and reestablishing the fellowship that sin had broken.

That same truth was spoken by Simeon, an elder Jew who was at the temple the day Mary and Joseph brought Jesus for presentation. Simeon had been told he wouldn't die until he saw the Christ Child. When he encountered Jesus, "he took Him up in his arms and blessed God and said: 'Lord, now You are letting Your servant depart in peace, according to Your word; for my eyes have seen Your salvation which You have prepared before the face of all peoples, a light to bring revelation to the Gentiles, and the glory of Your people Israel'" (Luke 2:28–32). Simeon's words gave insight into Jesus's specific purpose: to bring salvation not just to the Jews but to all people. And once Simeon saw the fulfillment of the promised Christ, he knew that he, too, was reconciled to God and had peace in Him.

Between the Last Supper and His arrest and crucifixion, Jesus promised His disciples, "Peace I leave with you, My peace I give to you; not as the world gives do I give to you. Let not your heart be troubled, neither let it be afraid" (John 14:27). Jesus makes it clear that His peace is something we'll never be able to find anywhere in the world—it only comes through faith in and fellowship with Him. And only He can give it to us.

Later in that same conversation, Jesus told them, "These things I have spoken to you, that in Me you may have peace. In the world you will have tribulation; but be of good cheer, I have overcome the world" (John 16:33). While struggle and strife in this world are a guarantee, so is the promise our Lord makes here—that no matter what happens, He is victorious.

After Jesus's death and resurrection, on Easter Sunday He appeared to the disciples, who were hiding in a room because they were afraid of the Jews. Suddenly, "Jesus came and stood in the midst, and said to them, 'Peace be with you'" (John 20:19). The disciples were undoubtedly anxious and uncertain about many things. So what did Jesus do? He came to them and declared peace. Jesus showed them His pierced hands and wounded side, and "then the disciples were glad when they saw the Lord" (John 20:20).

In his Epistle to the church in Rome, Paul wrote, "Therefore, having been justified by faith, we have peace with God through our Lord Jesus Christ, through whom also we have access by faith into this grace in which we stand, and rejoice in hope of the glory of God. And not only that, but we also glory in tribulations, knowing that tribulation produces perseverance; and perseverance, character; and character, hope" (Romans 5:1–4). When we are brought to faith in Christ—even when the world gives us plenty of reasons to be anxious—fears and doubts subside, as His peace becomes our peace.

Prayer

Heavenly Father, thank You for the peace we have with You and with one another in Christ Jesus, who "made peace through the blood of His cross" (Colossians 1:20). Help us to bring our concerns to You, and strengthen our hearts, daily reminding us of the hope we have in Jesus. And urge us to share this hope with our fellow Americans who struggle with anxiety and life's uncertainties. In His name we pray. Amen.

For Further Reflection

- Consider a time when a situation in the United States made you anxious or worried. Did you take that situation to the Lord? If not, how might you do this in the future?
- In a nation that's constantly experiencing different types of conflict and hardship, how can our responses to anxiety-inducing circumstances serve as a witness to the peace and hope we have in Jesus Christ?

____

____

____

____

____

____

Finding Hope Amid Disasters

The eyes of the Lord are on the righteous,
And His ears are open to their cry....
The righteous cry out, and the Lord hears,
And delivers them out of all their troubles.
The Lord is near to those who have a broken heart,
And saves such as have a contrite spirit.
Many are the afflictions of the righteous,
But the Lord delivers him out of them all.

—PSALM 34:15, 17–19

As we drove through the neighborhood surrounding our church, my eyes teared up at the devastation. Cars crushed, roofs torn off, trees completely uprooted, utility poles and lines downed... It looked like a scene out of an apocalyptic movie.

Lord, have mercy! was the only prayer I could find in that moment.

Massive, destructive tornadoes had torn through Tennessee and Kentucky, injuring dozens of people and killing several. The full extent of the damage was still being assessed, but the clean-up effort would obviously take time. However, reckoning with the mental and emotional toll this event had on individuals, families, and the community would undoubtedly take even more time.

Each year, the United States experiences numerous natural disasters. Wildfires, floods, hurricanes, tornadoes, earthquakes, mudslides, and other tragedies befall our people. We helplessly watch as first responders and rescue crews try to stem the tide of loss of life and property, and we despair over the rising death tolls in the daily headlines.

We call these types of events "natural disasters," but there's nothing "natural" about them. The Apostle Paul explained this in Romans 8:22: "For we know that the whole creation groans and labors with birth pangs together until now." Prior to humanity's fall into sin, creation was in perfect harmony. But afterward, everything was corrupted and thrust into a state of decay and turmoil. The chaos we see in nature reminds us of the reality of sin in the world.

When a disaster strikes, some think the people affected were stricken because of their sin. Jesus addressed this issue in Luke. After a tragic incident, He taught: "Those eighteen on whom the tower in Siloam fell and killed them, do you think that they were worse sinners than all other men who dwelt in Jerusalem? I tell you, no; but unless you repent you will all likewise perish" (Luke 13:4–5). Jesus's words make it clear that suffering isn't always a direct result of personal sin or divine judgment.

In another incident, Jesus once again corrected His disciples' misunderstanding about the relationship between personal sin and earthly struggles: "Now as Jesus passed by, He saw a man who was blind from birth. And His disciples asked Him, saying, 'Rabbi, who sinned, this man or his parents, that he was born blind?' Jesus answered, 'Neither this man nor his parents sinned, but that the works of God should be revealed in him'" (John 9:1–3). The man's suffering wasn't due to a specific sin. His ailment would be used as an occasion for Jesus to perform a miracle—not only to heal the man's blindness but also to save his soul.

When disasters hit home, it can be easy to feel forsaken. But Psalm 34:17–18 reminds us, "The righteous cry out, and the Lord hears and delivers them out of all their troubles. The Lord is near to those who have a broken heart." Even as we sit among the rubble of our homes, spend hour upon hour calling insurance companies and filling out forms, or mourn the loss of life, He is right there beside us, putting our sorrowful tears into His bottle (Psalm 56:8).

Christians have an opportunity to respond to tragedy in a way that reflects the confidence, trust, and hope we have in God, providing a powerful witness to the world. This is the kind of faith spoken of in the book of James: "My brethren, count it all joy when you fall into various trials, knowing that the testing of your faith produces patience. But let patience have its perfect work, that you may be perfect and complete, lacking nothing" (James 1:2–4).

During times of disaster, we also can come together as a community of believers to support our neighbors' physical and spiritual needs. We can volunteer for relief efforts, whether serving meals, handing out bottled water, distributing supplies, clearing debris, or repairing damaged buildings. We can listen to people share about how the event affected them and show empathy. And most importantly, we can share the Gospel of Jesus Christ with them.

In the days following the tornados, amid the tales of loss and heartbreak, other stories began to emerge—stories of healing and hope. A collection had been taken up to help a small-business owner get her store up and running anew. A stockpile of Christmas presents at a nonprofit for needy children had been spared. A four-month-old baby swept away from his destroyed home was later found safely nestled in a fallen tree. His family attributed his survival to God's grace.

Paul wrote, "For I consider that the sufferings of this present time are not worthy to be compared with the glory which shall be revealed in us. For the earnest expectation of the creation eagerly waits for the revealing of the sons of God. For the creation was subjected to futility, not willingly, but because of Him who subjected it in hope; because the creation itself also will be delivered from the bondage of corruption into the glorious liberty of the children of God" (Romans 8:18–21).

One day, Christ will return and make all things new, and natural disasters will no longer afflict the world. Until then, "let us hold fast the confession of our hope without wavering, for He who promised is faithful" (Hebrews 10:23).

Prayer

Dearest Lord, when natural disasters strike, we acutely feel the pain of living in a fallen world. In such times of trouble, help us remember that You are near to the brokenhearted, and You will deliver us from all our troubles. In the face of such tragedies, may our response to others reflect Your love and give hope to our communities. We ask this in Jesus's name. Amen.

For Further Reflection

- What would you say to someone who has lost everything in a catastrophic event like a hurricane, fire, flood, or tornado?
- How can you support your fellow Americans who have been afflicted by a natural disaster?

For You have promised, Lord,
to heed Your children's cries in time of need
Through Him whose name alone is great,
Our Savior and our advocate.

"When in the Hour of Deepest Need"

Leading with Zeal for the Lord

However You are just in all that has befallen us;
For You have dealt faithfully,
But we have done wickedly.
Neither our kings nor our princes,
Our priests nor our fathers,
Have kept Your law,
Nor heeded Your commandments and Your testimonies,
With which You testified against them.
For they have not served You in their kingdom,
Or in the many good things that You gave them,
Or in the large and rich land which You set before them;
Nor did they turn from their wicked works.

—NEHEMIAH 9:33–35

Nehemiah had his work cut out for him.

As the leader of the Jews who had returned to Jerusalem after the seventy-year Babylonian exile, he not only had the responsibility of rebuilding the city itself but also needed to restore faithful worship of the One True God.

Imagine what it was like for those who returned: Their formerly glorious city was in ruins, many decades after King Nebuchadnezzar had sacked and destroyed it, in fulfillment of the prophecy found in Jeremiah 25:8–9: "Therefore thus says the

Lord of hosts: 'Because you have not heard My words, behold, I will send and take all the families of the north,' says the Lord, 'and Nebuchadnezzar the king of Babylon, My servant, and will bring them against this land, against its inhabitants, and against these nations all around, and will utterly destroy them, and make them an astonishment, a hissing, and perpetual desolations.'"

In the siege, many Jews were killed, and survivors were scattered throughout the Babylonian Empire and forced into servitude. Some chose to intermarry and integrate within their new environments. The exiles were often prohibited from worshipping the Lord, as we read in books like Daniel, or they were in danger of being annihilated, as told in the book of Esther.

Because of everything that had happened, the Israelites lost both their homeland and their sense of national identity. Worst of all, they'd lost their place of worship and God's law—though one might posit they'd already lost the latter, which was why they were exiled in the first place.

Even so, the Lord was faithful, keeping His promise that He'd preserve a remnant that would one day return to Jerusalem: "But I will gather the remnant of My flock out of all countries where I have driven them, and bring them back to their folds; and they shall be fruitful and increase" (Jeremiah 23:3). Standing among the ruins and facing constant threats of violence from those who opposed the city's rebuilding, some of the Jews may have wondered—or even doubted altogether—if the desolate land could ever be fruitful again.

When things are going well for us, individually or nationally, we're often inclined to take the credit. *Look at all we've accomplished because of our hard work! See how blessed we are because we're such good people!*

Yet we must recognize the source of any and all blessings we receive, as people and as citizens: the Lord. Nehemiah said as much, when he told God that the Israelites "have not served You in their kingdom, or in the many good things that *You* gave them, or in the large and rich land which *You* set before them" (Nehemiah 9:35, emphasis added).

Alternately, when things go wrong, whether in our own lives or in our country, we sometimes want to blame God. Nehemiah rightly places the blame squarely where it belongs: *on us*. In his prayer, he lists every sector of society as being at fault: kings, princes, priests, and fathers. From the highest official of the realm to spiritual leaders and heads of households, the Israelites fell short in keeping God's law.

Can you see any parallels to the United States here?

Are America's civil leaders faithful in preserving our God-given rights, upholding peace, and punishing evildoers? Are America's pastors humble servants of the Word who teach the Gospel in purity and truth? Are America's fathers embracing their vocation, loving their wives as Christ loved the church and training their children to love and fear the Lord (Ephesians 5:25, 6:4)?

No, Israel isn't the only nation that has fallen short of God's standards.

After ensuring the completion of the city wall and reestablishing the people's covenant with the Lord, Nehemiah traveled to visit King Artaxerxes of Babylon. But when Nehemiah returned to Jerusalem, he discovered that some of his directives had either been ignored or overlooked. The Israelites started intermarrying with pagans, one of the priests had wrongly taken up residence in the temple, the people weren't providing material support for the temple, and the Sabbath was being violated. Basically, they picked up right where their exiled ancestors had left off.

Indeed, there's "nothing new under the sun" (Ecclesiastes 1:9).

And Nehemiah, though godly, was still a sinful human being. Upon his discovery of the Israelites' flagrant sins, he flew into a rage. At one point, he even attacked some of the transgressors: "So I contended with them and cursed them, struck some of them and pulled out their hair" (Nehemiah 13:25). While his manner of dealing with wrongdoing isn't necessarily something we should emulate, his passion for the Lord that prompted his actions reminds us of the words from Psalm 69:9: "zeal for Your house has eaten me up"—the same words cited in John 2:13–17 in reference to Jesus cleansing the temple.

None of our earthly rulers will ever be perfect, but we can still pray for the Lord to lift up steadfast leaders like Nehemiah, to guide us and remind us of God's faithfulness to us.

Prayer

Lord Almighty, at every level of society, whether civil or church leaders, citizens or congregants, we don't reach the standard You've set. Even though we're unfaithful to You, You're ever faithful to us. Allow us to daily reflect on how You mercifully provide leaders to guide us, and please place us under the authority of those who seek Your will. In the holy name of Jesus we pray. Amen.

For Further Reflection

- Can you think of any recent examples of times when our leaders—whether in our nation, workplace, homes, or anywhere else—have fallen short of the standard God has set for us? What kind of effect did these failures have on the people being led by these individuals?
- What leaders do you know who exemplify godly leadership? What characteristics do they exhibit? Pray for them to stay the course, and consider reaching out to thank them and tell them you're praying for them.

To God and to Caesar

And [the Pharisees] sent to Him their disciples with the Herodians, saying, "Teacher, we know that You are true, and teach the way of God in truth; nor do You care about anyone, for You do not regard the person of men. Tell us, therefore, what do You think? Is it lawful to pay taxes to Caesar, or not?"
But Jesus perceived their wickedness, and said, "Why do you test Me, you hypocrites? Show Me the tax money."
So they brought Him a denarius.
And He said to them, "Whose image and inscription is this?"
They said to Him, "Caesar's."
And He said to them, "Render therefore to Caesar the things that are Caesar's, and to God the things that are God's."

—MATTHEW 22:16–21

These days, it feels like we're drowning in taxes. Taxes on everyday necessities, like food, clothing, and gasoline. Property taxes. State and federal income taxes. Social Security taxes. Inheritance taxes. The list goes on and on.

We pay taxes, and then we struggle to make ends meet. Other times, we see how our tax dollars are being spent, and we get upset or frustrated. We might think, *How can the government be so irresponsible with my hard-earned money?* At certain points in our lives, we might have even considered not paying our taxes. After all, if the money is being used to fund things we disagree with, whether as a matter of principle or because it violates our Christian values, why should we knowingly contribute to those causes?

Such concerns are certainly valid, and we're blessed that the Bible speaks to these kinds of practical matters.

Matthew 22 takes place after Jesus's triumphal entry into Jerusalem on Palm Sunday, and after he cleansed the temple of the money changers and those selling animals for sacrifices. As was the custom for rabbis at that time, Jesus began teaching at the temple. In His typical fashion, many of the lessons were presented as parables.

The prominent Jewish sects of the day, the Sadducees and Pharisees, began interrogating Jesus about many different subjects, trying to trick Him into either blaspheming against God, so they could punish Him for that offense, or speaking against the Roman Empire, so they could report Him to the authorities for punishment.

This scene wasn't the first time Jesus had been questioned about taxes. Earlier in Matthew, the temple leaders in Capernaum had approached Peter and asked him whether Jesus paid the temple tax. Peter said yes without hesitation.

Upon entering the house where Jesus was visiting, He asked Peter a question: "What do you think, Simon? From whom do the kings of the earth take customs or taxes, from their sons or from strangers?" (Matthew 17:25). Peter answered, "From strangers." Jesus then said, "Then the sons are free. Nevertheless, lest we offend them, go to the sea, cast in a hook, and take the fish that comes up first. And when you have opened its mouth, you will find a piece of money; take that and give it to them for Me and you" (Matthew 17:27). (For whatever reason, I've always found it both hilarious and fascinating that Jesus used this miracle to provide the money for their temple tax. It's one of many stories I'd love to hear from Him and Peter one day.)

Jesus is God, and He is the temple. Thus, He's certainly under no obligation to pay the temple tax. Nevertheless, He was committed to keeping and fulfilling the law perfectly on our behalf, so we wouldn't be eternally punished for something impossible for us to do.

In Jesus's explanation, He subtly communicated to Peter that a new order was being established. Jesus proclaimed, "My kingdom is not of this world" (John 18:36). With Him as our eternal King, we're no longer under any law that says we must pay a temple tax. Of course, this doesn't mean we abstain from financially supporting our church—it merely means that we do so cheerfully in gratitude to God, recognizing that all we have is from Him and truly belongs to Him, and that contributing to the work of the church furthers His heavenly kingdom (2 Corinthians 9:7).

At times we might disagree with the way our tithes are spent. Undoubtedly, both Jesus and Peter may have disagreed with how the temple taxes were being used. But they paid them anyway, and we should do the same.

So it also goes with our civil tax dollars, and the times we might feel that our government wastes these tax dollars.

When the Pharisees and Herodians tried to trick Jesus, He already knew their sinful motivation in questioning Him, in spite of prefacing their question with flattery. Jesus knows every person's heart, and He didn't hesitate to call out their deceit: "Why do you test Me, you hypocrites?" (Matthew 22:18). He told them to show Him the tax money, which was a different coin than the one used for the temple tax.

Then He asked them, "Whose image and inscription is this?" (Matthew 22:20). Jesus was a master of the Socratic method, asking questions to stimulate critical thinking and deepen His listeners' understanding of theological teachings. However, His questioners may have been wondering, *Why is He asking us this? Can't He see the image and inscription with His own eyes?*

Regardless, they answered His question and said, "Caesar's." He then told them to "Render therefore to Caesar the things that are Caesar's, and to God the things that are God's" (Matthew 22:21).

In his response, Jesus established a couple of fundamental truths about the relationship between Christians and civil authorities. First, He recognized the legitimacy of civil government and our responsibility to it as citizens. This is part of the divine order God established to maintain peace and administer justice here on earth. Christians are called to honor leaders, obey civil laws, and contribute to society—and paying taxes fulfills all of these commitments.

Second, He emphasized that we must give to God what is God's. Yet what is God's? The short answer to this question is:

everything. But what is Jesus referring to in the context of this passage?

If we're to render unto Caesar what bears his image, then we're to render unto God what bears His image—and that's *us*.

Genesis 1:26–27 says: "'Let Us make man in Our image, according to Our likeness....' So God created man in His own image; in the image of God He created him; male and female He created them." Every human being is inscribed with God's image, which means that our ultimate allegiance is to Him and Him only.

While we submit to civil authorities as commanded by God, we must guard against compromising our faith and values in the process. Our highest calling in the context of our citizenship is continuing to live out our faith and reflect God's heavenly kingdom in thought, word, and deed.

Prayer

Dear Lord, as long as we're citizens of two kingdoms—heaven and earth—we'll experience the tension that comes with being in the world but not of the world (John 17:16). Please give us peace as we navigate this tension, allowing us to submit to our civil authorities while recognizing and acknowledging Your dominion over all things in both kingdoms. May we render unto You all that is Yours. In Your Son Jesus Christ's name we pray. Amen.

For Further Reflection

- Reflect on your civic responsibilities. Are there areas where you might be neglecting your duties? Recognize these as opportunities to honor God and the structures He has erected to keep order in our society.
- Have you ever experienced tension or confusion between what must be rendered to Caesar and what must be rendered to God? If so, pray for the Lord to grant you wisdom and clarity in the situation, so you may honor God first and foremost.

Teach the Children Diligently

*You shall love the Lord your God with all your heart,
with all your soul, and with all your strength.
And these words which I command you today shall be in
your heart. You shall teach them diligently to your children,
and shall talk of them when you sit in your house, when you walk
by the way, when you lie down, and when you rise up.
You shall bind them as a sign on your hand, and they shall
be as frontlets between your eyes. You shall write them on the
doorposts of your house and on your gates.*

—DEUTERONOMY 6:5–9

Did anyone instruct you in God's law when you were a child? Some of us were raised in a belief other than Christianity. Some of us may have been raised in a "Christian" home and attended church on Sundays as long as we didn't have something else on the schedule. And some of us were blessed to be raised in strong Christian homes, where the Lord truly was the centerpiece of the family.

Of all these scenarios, only one demonstrates the Lord's commands as expressed in today's verses from Deuteronomy: the ones where God is integrated into every aspect of family life.

In verse 5, the Lord admonishes you to love Him "with all your heart, with all your soul, and with all your strength." The love of the Lord is to be our first and foremost passion, preoccupation, and pursuit. It's the nucleus of our lives, and all that we say, do, think, and feel should revolve around it.

And we should note the juxtaposition of verses 5 and 6, when the latter verse says, "These words which I command you today shall be in your heart." Notice the repetition of "heart." How do we love the Lord our God? By keeping His law.

In giving us His law and writing it on our hearts, God demonstrates His fatherly love for us (Jeremiah 31:33; Hebrews 8:10). He's not some big, cosmic meanie who doesn't want us to have any fun—He wants to protect us from things that will harm us, both temporally and eternally.

In many ways, this is no different from earthly parents. Because they love us, they establish rules for us, to protect us and teach us right from wrong. You'd be hard-pressed to find someone who thinks that parents who have no rules for their children are loving. (I say this as someone who grew up in a household with few rules and minimal parenting. Though I was the envy of all my friends—*No bedtime? No chores? How wonderful!*—I can assure you that the outcomes were less than ideal.)

Yes, earthly parents are imperfect, which means their rules can be imperfect too. And as children, at times we obeyed them because we feared punishment. The same can be true of our obedience to the Heavenly Father. But such is life in a sinful, fallen world. In a perfect world, we'd always obey God and our parents out of love for them.

Jesus Himself modeled perfect obedience for us in His relationship with both His earthly parents and His Heavenly Father.

In Luke 2, twelve-year-old Jesus and His family traveled to Jerusalem for the feast. When Mary and Joseph headed home, they accidentally left Jesus behind because they thought He was among the family group they were traveling in. If you've ever "lost" your child, you can imagine their stress level.

They returned to Jerusalem and found Jesus in the temple, engaging with the teachers. Mary said to Him, "Son, why have you done this to us? Look, Your father and I have sought You anxiously" (Luke 2:48). To which Jesus responded, "Why did you seek Me? Did you not know that I must be about My Father's business?" (Luke 2:49). Jesus offered a gentle correction to Mary's rebuke, though his parents "did not understand the statement which He spoke to them" (Luke 2:50). After that, "He went down with them and came to Nazareth, and was subject to them" (Luke 2:51).

At the end of His life, Jesus displayed definitive and perfect obedience to the Father, as "He humbled Himself and became obedient to the point of death, even the death of the cross" (Philippians 2:8).

Jesus was the only One who ever kept God's law perfectly. And though in this age we'll never be able to do as our Savior did, that doesn't mean we shouldn't learn God's law and hold it in the forefront of our minds at all times, to guide our lives with God and other people. As Jesus told His disciples, "He who has My commandments and keeps them, it is he who loves Me. And he who loves Me will be loved by My Father, and I will love him and manifest Myself to him" (John 14:21).

However, God doesn't want us to stop with our own instruction in His law—He tells us to "teach them to [our] children" (Deuteronomy 11:19). And we're to do this throughout the day, anywhere and everywhere. In our modern life, this might look like reciting the Ten Commandments and other Bible verses in the car on the way to and from school or sports practice. Perhaps it's singing hymns while you make dinner together in the kitchen. Listening to an audio Bible on road trips. Saying a prayer together before everyone leaves the house in the morning, and closing the day by praying together.

The world wants more than anything to distract us and our children from God and His Word. The culture, media, peer influences, electronic devices, extracurricular activities, and many other forces strive to steal our time, attention, hearts, and minds away from the Lord.

If we want our children to learn to love the Lord and His law, we must be fierce and intentional about it, weaving these practices into the ebb and flow of our daily lives. As parents, we shouldn't outsource our children's spiritual formation to anyone else, whether pastors, Sunday school teachers, or parochial schoolteachers. While each of these individuals can supplement the instruction we provide our children, they should never replace it. The Lord has given our children to *us*—we have the foremost responsibility to teach them to love the Lord with all their heart, soul, and strength.

Our children are the future of our country. If we want strong, Christ-centered people leading our nation for many generations to come, we must *raise* these leaders. This isn't something that will happen by accident. Today, let's make a conscious choice to give our children the spiritual foundation they need, so that when their faith is tested, they'll be able to stand up under it (1 Corinthians 10:13).

Prayer

Heavenly Father, Your law is a beautiful reflection of Your character, and it teaches us how to live with You and with other people. Please give us the wisdom, patience, and tenacity to instruct our children in Your ways, so they may learn to love You and Your law. May our homes be a place where we honor Your commandments, as You help us cultivate love and resilience in the face of the world's trials. Amen.

For Further Reflection

- As a family, what practices can you adopt that will instill a love of God and His Word in your children or grandchildren? You can even answer this question as a family. After you've compiled a list of options, choose at least one activity to start today.
- Think of a godly leader you admire, past or present. If possible, do some research about that person's childhood. What, if any, spiritual practices did their parents do regularly to help shape them into the person they became? In what ways can this inspire you and your family?

Strong Shepherds, Strong Flocks

The weak you have not strengthened, nor have you healed those who were sick, nor bound up the broken, nor brought back what was driven away, nor sought what was lost; but with force and cruelty you have ruled them. So they were scattered because there was no shepherd; and they became food for all the beasts of the field when they were scattered. My sheep wandered through all the mountains, and on every high hill; yes, My flock was scattered over the whole face of the earth, and no one was seeking or searching for them.

—EZEKIEL 34:4–6

Throughout the Old Testament, especially in the prophetical books, some of God's harshest rebukes were directed at the priests.

Israel's religious leaders were all descended from Levi, one of the patriarch Jacob's twelve sons. During the forty years of desert wandering after the Exodus from Egypt, the Lord instructed His people about proper worship. He also instructed them regarding the tribes' land allotments within the territory God had vowed to one day give Abraham's descendants.

All of the tribes, except Levi, received an allotment.

Instead, the Levites were scattered throughout the land and given the awesome duty of serving the Lord at the tabernacle where the Israelites worshipped. And one day, they'd serve at the temple Solomon built in Jerusalem. Exodus, Leviticus, Numbers, and Deuteronomy all include details about the tabernacle, including the priestly duties.

The Lord said the following to Moses regarding the Levites: "So you shall bring the Levites before the Lord, and the children of Israel shall lay their hands on the Levites; and Aaron shall offer the Levites before the Lord like a wave offering from the children of Israel, that they may perform the work of the Lord.... Thus you shall separate the Levites from among the children of Israel, and the Levites shall be Mine.... For they are wholly given to Me from among the children of Israel; I have taken them for Myself instead of all who open the womb, the firstborn of all the children of Israel" (Numbers 8:10–11, 14, 16).

The Levites were tasked not only with serving at the tabernacle by offering sacrifices to atone for sin but also with teaching the people the Lord's law (Deuteronomy 33:10).

Moses and his older brother, Aaron, were both from the tribe of Levi. Aaron became Israel's first high priest, and his sons would take on that role after him. It was a humbling task to serve as intermediary between God and His people, and not something to be taken lightly. Aaron's sons Nadab and Abihu learned this lesson quickly, when they offered "profane fire before the Lord," and "fire went out from the Lord and devoured them, and they died before the Lord" (Leviticus 10:1–2). God's law reflected His holiness and was to be obeyed without exception.

From the time the Israelites entered the Promised Land, they struggled to keep God's law, and the priests often fell short in their duties to instruct, admonish, and encourage the people. When the Israelites became spiritually weak and sick, the priests didn't call them to repentance with the truth of God's law. When the people were brokenhearted, the priests neglected to remind them of the Lord's unfailing love. When the people's sin drove them from God, the priests didn't pursue them, find them, and bring them back to the fold. Even worse, they were flat-out cruel.

Many of the minor prophets' writings detail the priests' failures. One prophecy against their failures says, "Thus says the Lord my God, 'Feed the flock for slaughter, whose owners slaughter them and feel no guilt; those who sell them say, "Blessed be the Lord, for I am rich"; and their shepherds do not pity them'" (Zechariah 11:4–5). The priests were more concerned with their own wealth and well-being than the sheep entrusted to them.

Therefore, the flock was scattered—first, spiritually, as they slid into apostasy and idolatry, and then literally, when Israel's Northern and Southern Kingdoms were exiled to Assyria and Babylon, respectively.

When the Jews returned to the land decades later, they set about rebuilding the temple: "But many of the priests and Levites and heads of the fathers' houses, old men who had seen the first temple, wept with a loud voice when the foundation of this temple was laid before their eyes" (Ezra 3:12). Their tears were undoubtedly bittersweet—rejoicing that they had returned to the land yet mourning over what had been lost. And perhaps the priests and Levites, in particular, rued having neglected their duties.

Hundreds of years later, the Israelites' shepherd situation hadn't improved much. Jesus also rebuked the Levites and priests during His visible ministry, for many of the same reasons the Old Testament prophets had condemned the religious leaders of their day. For instance, in Matthew, He said, "But woe to you, scribes and Pharisees, hypocrites! For you shut up the kingdom of heaven against men; for you neither go in yourselves, nor do you allow those who are entering to go in. Woe to you, scribes and Pharisees, hypocrites! For you devour widows' houses, and for a pretense make long prayers. Therefore you will receive greater condemnation" (Matthew 23:13–14).

Jesus doesn't mince words when addressing these religious leaders. His love and compassion for the sheep was too great, as He is "the good shepherd" who "gives His life for the sheep" (John 10:11).

In Luke 12:48, Jesus said, "For everyone to whom much is given, from him much will be required; and to whom much has been committed, of him they will ask the more." The religious leaders had an awesome responsibility to serve God's people through their preaching and teaching. They were held to a higher standard, and God Himself expected more from them, as James wrote: "My brethren, let not many of you become teachers, knowing that we shall receive a stricter judgment" (James 3:1).

Jesus traveled to different locations as He was "teaching in their synagogues, preaching the gospel of the kingdom, and healing every sickness and every disease among the people" (Matthew 9:35). In every way that the priests had failed the people, Jesus was perfect. Unlike many of the Old Testament and New Testament priests who were cruel to the people, Jesus had compassion for the people "because they were weary and scattered, like sheep having no shepherd" (Matthew 9:36). He then encouraged His disciples to pray that God would send out laborers into His harvest (Matthew 9:38).

Jesus is our Good Shepherd, and we are the sheep of His pasture (Psalm 100:3). He is the fulfillment of what David wrote in Psalm 23:3: "He restores my soul; He leads me in the paths of righteousness for His name's sake." While we walk this earth, He has entrusted us to the care of His undershepherds, our pastors.

As we navigate the struggles and complexities of modern life in our nation, we need strong, Christ-centered pastors. Being a pastor is more than a job—it's a divine commission. Pastors are called to lovingly serve God's sheep through effective teaching, sound preaching, and right administering of the sacraments. We need church leaders who are committed to these holy tasks, offering the pure Gospel without compromising biblical truth—regardless of any pressure they receive from civil authorities.

Let us pray for and encourage our shepherds in their calling, as we seek to serve and obey our Lord Jesus Christ.

Prayer

Lord Almighty, we are so grateful to You for blessing us with shepherds to serve and minister to Your sheep. May You continually bless the work of their hands, that the church in our nation is strengthened and more sheep may be brought into the pasture of the Good Shepherd, Jesus Christ. Honor, praise, and glory be to Him forevermore. Amen.

For Further Reflection

- Have you ever experienced conflict with one of your shepherds? How did it affect your relationship with him? Did it affect your fellowship with God in any way?
- In what ways can you support your shepherd in his ministry?

O Comforter of priceless worth,
Send peace and unity on earth;
Support us in our final strife
And lead us out of death to life.

"Lord, Keep Us Steadfast in Your Word"

Work as to the Lord

And whatever you do, do it heartily, as to the Lord and not to men, knowing that from the Lord you will receive the reward of the inheritance; for you serve the Lord Christ.

—COLOSSIANS 3:23–24

Most of us have had more than one job in our lifetime, and many of us have had several. I daresay that most of us have had a job that we'd rather forget—maybe because the work was monotonous, we experienced conflict with a coworker or boss, or we weren't fairly compensated for our time and effort.

Yet some of our jobs have been a joy, whether it was because we liked the work itself, had great relationships with coworkers, or had a boss who mentored us and helped us grow professionally and personally.

In the United States, our identities are often wrapped up in our job titles. This is especially evident at social gatherings. When you meet someone, often the first question asked is "So, what do you do for a living?" We feel that knowing what someone does for work can tell us something about them, such as their interests, skills, and personality.

Though the idea might be inconceivable to us, work was never intended to be burdensome. When God created the world, He also instituted work as part of His perfect design. We're told that "The Lord God planted a garden eastward in Eden, and there He put the man whom He had formed.... Then the Lord God took the man and put him in the garden of Eden to tend and keep it" (Genesis 2:8, 15). Originally, work was meant to be a source of joy and fulfillment, a way for mankind to exercise stewardship over the Lord's beautiful creation.

Sadly, this blessed perfection didn't last. After Adam and Eve ate the fruit from the tree of the knowledge of good and evil, God handed down punishments, telling Adam specifically, "Cursed is the ground for your sake; in toil you shall eat of it all the days of your life. Both thorns and thistles it shall bring forth for you, and you shall eat the herb of the field. In the sweat of your face you shall eat bread till you return to the ground, for out of it you were taken; for dust you are, and to dust you shall return" (Genesis 3:17–19).

Because of sin, the ground itself was transformed from a place of abundant provision, where the Lord "made every tree grow that is pleasant to the sight and good for food," into a place of scarcity, where in spite of Adam's labors it would yield "thorns and thistles" (Genesis 2:9, 3:18). Work remained essential for survival because it provided food, but it wouldn't necessarily be enjoyable.

Work can be mentally, physically, and emotionally exhausting. However, idleness isn't a suitable antidote to these difficulties. Proverbs 21:25–26 issues the following warning:

“The desire of the lazy man kills him, for his hands refuse to labor. He covets greedily all day long, but the righteous gives and does not spare.” God had commanded the Israelites to care for the widows, orphans, and other needy people in their midst; able-bodied men were expected to work.

Yet as we see in these verses from Proverbs, men could be more inclined to covet what others had instead of earning for themselves, explicitly breaking God’s commandments.

In the New Testament, Paul wrote a similar admonition to the church at Thessalonica: “For even when we were with you, we commanded you this: If anyone will not work, neither shall he eat. For we hear that there are some who walk among you in a disorderly manner, not working at all, but are busybodies. Now those who are such we command and exhort through our Lord Jesus Christ that they work in quietness and eat their own bread” (2 Thessalonians 3:10–12). Paul chastises some of the saints for being idle and wasting time by gossiping and being more concerned with others’ affairs than with working.

Based on earlier verses, it also seems that they were eating bread that others had earned: “For you yourselves know how you ought to follow us, for we were not disorderly among you; nor did we eat anyone’s bread free of charge, but worked with labor and toil night and day, that we might not be a burden to any of you, not because we do not have authority, but to make ourselves an example of how you should follow us” (2 Thessalonians 3:7–9). Paul reminded his readers that he and his brothers had earned their keep while doing their mission work (his trade was tentmaking, as mentioned in Acts 18:3), to set an example for the other believers.

Scripture shows that work is integral to both a thriving society and a healthy church. As it says in Psalm 128:2, "When you eat the labor of your hands, you shall be happy, and it shall be well with you." Particularly in the body of Christ, work should be a priority. Refusing to do so demonstrates not only a disregard for the blessing of work itself but also for our God-given talents and the ability to support ourselves and our family.

Of course, some people are unable to work, perhaps due to physical impairment. And other people, such as mothers who stay home with their children, choose not to be in the labor force. But these aren't the types of people being addressed in these verses from Proverbs and 2 Thessalonians.

The crux of the matter is our heart. Our work, no matter what we do for a living, is an opportunity to glorify God, as we serve and love our neighbors through the labor of our hands. In each responsibility and task before us on any given day—from household chores and caregiving to team projects and presentations—we serve as Christ's ambassadors. Every duty, when undertaken with thanksgiving to the Lord, gains eternal significance.

Because we're sinful, at times we're ungrateful for our jobs. Other times, our jobs can become idols that steal us away from our God-given responsibilities and priorities. When we're disgruntled with our jobs, we might complain, cut corners, or not complete tasks to the best of our abilities. We grow weary and resent having to work hard, or we wish we earned more money or had a more prestigious title. In those moments, we can repent and seek forgiveness. We also can remember these verses from Colossians, which remind us that every task, big or small, carries profound significance when we do it unto Him.

A nation full of hardworking people truly is a blessing, providing the backbone of a robust economy, which can be a rising tide that lifts all ships.

Though we Christians find our identity in Christ, the talents and skills He's given us are part of how we're "fearfully and wonderfully made" (Psalm 139:14). When we joyfully labor and appreciate the significance of our work, knowing that it's not done in vain if done for the Lord, we can encourage and inspire everyone around us.

And who knows? Maybe one day, a coworker, customer, or client will ask you about your joyful approach to work, and you can share the "reason for the hope that is in you"—the salvation you have in the Lord Jesus Christ, whom you serve and from whom you'll receive an eternal inheritance (1 Peter 3:15).

Prayer

Gracious Lord, You have blessed us with unique talents and skills that we can put to use in our labors, whatever they may be, to bring honor and glory to Your holy name. Forgive us for the times we haven't appreciated this blessing or recognized that our labors give us opportunities to serve our Lord Jesus Christ, love our neighbor, and share the Gospel. Please help us to do our work with joy and with thanksgiving, in Jesus's name. Amen.

For Further Reflection

- How often do you pray about your work? If you're not in this habit, consider writing a prayer that you can read each day before you begin the work God has prepared in advance for you to do.
- Every day, we encounter people who are working hard—cashiers, mail carriers, servers, teachers, stay-at-home moms, nurses, and so forth. Consider how you could show your appreciation for these individuals, encouraging them in their labors and asking the Lord to bless the work of their hands.

The Heart of a King

The king's heart is in the hand of the Lord,
Like the rivers of water;
He turns it wherever He wishes.

—PROVERBS 21:1

Everywhere in the world, rivers are a source of life. In addition to providing fresh water for humans and animals alike, they contain food sources like fish, and for millennia, farmers have used rivers to irrigate their crops, further nourishing the living beings in the vicinity. Civilizations tend to spring up around rivers, as any population density map will show you.

Although human beings are able to harness the power of rivers, whether for industry, agriculture, or recreation, God has ultimate control over the river itself—where it flows, whether it dries up or overflows, how fast the waters travel, and so forth.

And so it is with the hearts of kings and other civil leaders, which God Himself also directs.

One of the most well-known and prominent biblical examples of this is Pharaoh, king of Egypt. During the time of the Exodus, God said to Moses prior to his first meeting with Pharaoh, "You shall speak all that I command you. And Aaron your brother shall tell Pharaoh to send the children of Israel out of his land. And I will harden Pharaoh's heart, and multiply My signs and My wonders in the land of Egypt. But Pharaoh will not heed you, so that I may lay My hand on Egypt and bring My armies and My people, the children of Israel, out of the land of Egypt by great judgments. And the Egyptians shall know that I am the Lord, when I stretch out My hand on Egypt and bring out the children of Israel from among them" (Exodus 7:2–5). From the onset, the Lord made it clear that He would harden Pharaoh's heart, so that He would be glorified.

Moses and Aaron went before Pharaoh to request that the Israelites be allowed to leave Egypt. God had told the brothers to perform a miracle, turning Aaron's rod into a serpent. However, Pharaoh's magicians replicated this miracle, even though Aaron's serpent devoured the magicians' serpents, demonstrating God's greater power. In spite of this, "Pharaoh's heart grew hard, and he did not heed them, as the Lord had said" (Exodus 7:13).

When the Nile River was turned to blood, "the magicians of Egypt did so with their enchantments; and Pharaoh's heart grew hard, and he did not heed them, as the Lord had said. And Pharaoh turned and went into his house. Neither was his heart moved by this" (Exodus 7:22–23). After each of the ten plagues, that became the refrain: Pharaoh's heart was hardened. His subjects were suffering mightily, and after the eighth plague, they implored him to let the Israelites go. It's a sad reality when leaders can be stubborn and prideful, regardless of the detrimental impact their decisions have on the people.

Note the progression regarding the hardening of Pharaoh's heart. After the first through the fifth plagues, Pharaoh hardened his own heart, but after the sixth plague, "the Lord hardened the heart of Pharaoh; and he did not heed them, just as the Lord had spoken to Moses" (Exodus 9:12). Paul wrote of the hardening of hearts in Romans 1:20–23, and although he was writing to first-century Christians, his words apply to Pharaoh as well: "For since the creation of the world His invisible attributes are clearly seen, being understood by the things that are made, even His eternal power and Godhead, so that they are without excuse, because, although they knew God, they did not glorify Him as God, nor were thankful, but became futile in their thoughts, and their foolish hearts were darkened. Professing to be wise, they became fools, and changed the glory of the incorruptible God into an image made like corruptible man—and birds and four-footed animals and creeping things."

Ever since man was formed from the dust of the earth, the One True God had revealed Himself in creation to all people, including Pharaoh and the rest of the Egyptians. But instead of worshipping the Creator, they "exchanged the truth of God for the lie, and worshiped and served the creature rather than the Creator" (Romans 1:25). The Egyptians were prolific worshippers of the created, making idols out of the sun, the Nile River, frogs, insects, snakes, and many other things. The Lord's judgment of Egypt was not only against their leader and his subjects but also against their false gods, as each one of the plagues undermined these idols.

In contrast to Pharaoh was Cyrus, king of Persia. Although he, too, was pagan, God referred to him as His shepherd and "His anointed" (Isaiah 45:1). Isaiah prophesied that one day—which turned out to be 150 years later—this ruler would be used as an instrument to accomplish God's will: "He is My shepherd, and he shall perform all My pleasure, saying to Jerusalem, 'You shall be built,' and to the temple, 'Your foundation shall be laid.' Thus says the Lord to His anointed, to Cyrus, whose right hand I have held—to subdue nations before him and loose the armor of kings, to open before him the double doors, so that the gates will not be shut.... I have raised him up in righteousness, and I will direct all his ways; He shall build My city and let My exiles go free, not for price nor reward" (Isaiah 44:28–45:1, 13).

We read about the fulfillment of this prophecy in Ezra 1:1–2: "Now in the first year of Cyrus king of Persia, that the word of the Lord by the mouth of Jeremiah might be fulfilled, the Lord stirred up the spirit of Cyrus king of Persia, so that he made a proclamation throughout all his kingdom, and also put it in writing, saying, Thus says Cyrus king of Persia: All the kingdoms of the earth the Lord God of heaven has given me. And He has commanded me to build Him a house at Jerusalem which is in Judah."

Even though Cyrus was an unbeliever, God moved him to allow His people to return to the Promised Land, so they could rebuild the city and the temple after the seventy years of the Babylonian exile were complete.

Daniel 2:21 says that the Lord "changes the times and the seasons; He removes kings and raises up kings; He gives wisdom to the wise and knowledge to those who have understanding." Whether our leaders are resisting God, like Pharaoh, or following His prompting, like Cyrus, we can trust that in either situation, He is actively working, influencing their hearts and directing their steps, to align their paths with His divine purposes.

Prayer

Thank You, Heavenly Father, that You hold the heart of every person in Your hands, including our leaders, and guide them according to Your perfect, gracious will. Please help us cling to this truth even when circumstances seem uncertain, and to faithfully pray for our leaders, so Your purposes may be fulfilled in our country. In Jesus's name we pray. Amen.

For Further Reflection

- Does knowing that the hearts of our political leaders are in the Lord's hands alter your perception of them? Why or why not?
- If our leaders were to acknowledge that God was in control, how do you think that would affect their decision-making?

For Such a Time as This

And Mordecai told them to answer Esther: "Do not think in your heart that you will escape in the king's palace any more than all the other Jews. For if you remain completely silent at this time, relief and deliverance will arise for the Jews from another place, but you and your father's house will perish. Yet who knows whether you have come to the kingdom for such a time as this?"

—ESTHER 4:13–14

Imagine that one day, the president of the United States meets with one of his cabinet members. The secretary informs him there's a group of people in the country that refuses to obey the laws of the land. In spite of economic, social, and legal pressures, these individuals hold fast to their beliefs and values. The secretary says that, in the interest of preventing this group from causing disturbances throughout the land, they should be eliminated. And if this is accomplished, a powerful donor has agreed to contribute a sizeable amount to the president's reelection campaign.

This all sounds good to the president, and with the flourish of his pen, he signs an executive order commanding that all Christians be executed.

Thanks be to God that such things aren't possible in our constitutional republic, where our system includes checks and balances between the different branches of government to prevent both tyranny and mob rule.

However, this is the exact situation that was faced by the exiled Jews living in the Persian Empire during the reign of King Ahasuerus (also known as Xerxes).

Not long before the decree was enacted to kill all the Jews, King Ahasuerus had promoted Haman the Agagite "and set his seat above all the princes who were with him" (Esther 3:1). In addition to this, "all the king's servants who were within the king's gate bowed and paid homage to Haman, for so the king had commanded concerning him. But Mordecai would not bow or pay homage" (Esther 3:2).

Mordecai was a relative of King Ahasuerus's queen, Esther. She'd been orphaned, and Mordecai raised her as his daughter. She'd come to her position after the former queen, Vashti, refused to go before the king and was therefore deposed.

Before Esther became queen, Mordecai had told her not to reveal her Jewish heritage. It may have been that Mordecai feared people would use that knowledge against her, since the Jews, while enjoying a level of freedom in the Persian Empire, were still essentially captives.

Mordecai sat at the king's gate, which indicates he likely held some civil authority because much of the city's business was conducted there. This position also would have given him access to the powerful and influential people who were present.

We're never told why Mordecai refused to bow to Haman, but we learn the result: "When Haman saw that Mordecai did not bow or pay him homage, Haman was filled with wrath. But he disdained to lay hands on Mordecai alone, for they had told him of the people of Mordecai. Instead, Haman sought to destroy all the Jews who were throughout the whole kingdom of Ahasuerus—the people of Mordecai" (Esther 3:5–6).

Haman then hatched an insidious plot. He went to King Ahasuerus and said, "There is a certain people scattered and dispersed among the people in all the provinces of your kingdom; their laws are different from all other people's, and they do not keep the king's laws. Therefore it is not fitting for the king to let them remain. If it pleases the king, let a decree be written that they be destroyed, and I will pay ten thousand talents of silver into the hands of those who do the work, to bring it into the king's treasuries" (Esther 3:8–9).

When Mordecai heard this news, "he tore his clothes and put on sackcloth and ashes, and went out into the midst of the city. He cried out with a loud and bitter cry" (Esther 4:1). Esther heard about Mordecai's distress and sent one of her attendants to discover the reason for her adoptive father's anguish. Along with sharing the decree with her, Mordecai hoped that Esther would "go in to the king to make supplication to him and plead before him for her people" (Esther 4:8).

But Esther was reticent. She hadn't been called to go in to the king for a month, and anyone who went unbidden before the king would be executed.

Mordecai didn't accept her response, telling her through messengers, "Do not think in your heart that you will escape in the king's palace any more than all the other Jews. For if you remain completely silent at this time, relief and deliverance will arise for the Jews from another place, but you and your father's house will perish. Yet who knows whether you have come to the kingdom for such a time as this?" (Esther 4:13–14). His words seemed to hearten Esther and help her understand what was truly at stake—both the lives of the Jews and her own life.

She then agreed to help: "Go, gather all the Jews who are present in Shushan, and fast for me; neither eat nor drink for three days, night or day. My maids and I will fast likewise. And so I will go to the king, which is against the law; and if I perish, I perish!" (Esther 4:16).

Esther successfully went before the king, and she shrewdly revealed Haman's plot, as well as her Jewish heritage. Haman was executed, and King Ahasuerus elevated Mordecai to Haman's former position.

Because Persian royal decrees were irrevocable, Mordecai wrote a new decree, declaring that the Jews could defend themselves from anyone who sought to harm them (Esther 8:11–12). They did so, and that day became a Jewish festival named Purim, which is still celebrated today.

The book concludes with these words: "For Mordecai the Jew was second to King Ahasuerus, and was great among the Jews and well received by the multitude of his brethren, seeking the good of his people and speaking peace to all his countrymen" (Esther 10:3).

Throughout the book of Esther, we see how God uses individuals in positions of power and influence to serve His purposes. Mordecai's words to Esther remind us that remaining silent in the face of injustice is unacceptable for those who fear and love God. Instead, we're to act with courage and conviction.

Christians have both the opportunity and responsibility to influence laws and civil authorities so that they align with God's love and justice. Jesus says we are to love our neighbors as ourselves (Matthew 22:39). This love should extend to how we engage with the civil realm, including government. We can advocate for just laws, defend the oppressed, lobby for policies that uphold biblical truth, run for office, and campaign for candidates we feel best represent our Christian beliefs and values.

Even when we're performing these duties, our ultimate allegiance is to the Lord and His truth, and we do what He requires of us: "to do justly, to love mercy, and to walk humbly with [our] God" (Micah 6:8). Our actions can have far-reaching implications, and if we find ourselves in a position of power in the civil realm, we should ensure that our influence points others to the truth of Jesus Christ.

Prayer

Lord Almighty, You know all things, including when You have placed us in certain positions "for such a time as this," just like your faithful servants Esther and Mordecai. Thank You for opportunities that You have provided for us to influence our communities and government, to honor You and serve our neighbors. When we engage with the civil realm, may You grant us the courage to stand firm in Your truth. In Jesus's name we pray. Amen.

For Further Reflection

- Why do you think some Christians feel that believers shouldn't be involved in the civil realm? Does that idea align with Scripture? Why or why not?
- Have you ever been able to influence someone in a position of power, or were you ever in such a position yourself? If so, how did your knowledge of God's truth guide your actions?

The Rejection of Knowledge

Hear the word of the Lord,
You children of Israel,
For the Lord brings a charge against the inhabitants of the land:
"There is no truth or mercy
Or knowledge of God in the land.
By swearing and lying,
Killing and stealing and committing adultery,
They break all restraint,
With bloodshed upon bloodshed....
"My people are destroyed for lack of knowledge.
Because you have rejected knowledge,
I also will reject you from being priest for Me;
Because you have forgotten the law of your God,
I also will forget your children."

—HOSEA 4:1–2, 6

In our modern world, we have access to more information than ever before. The internet has become so vast that you could spend several lifetimes exploring it and never reach the end. Anything and everything you want to know about, no matter how obscure, is at your fingertips—just grab your ever-present smartphone and look it up.

But has this increased access to information led to increased knowledge, especially knowledge of the Lord?

All you need to do is look at the moral and spiritual landscape of the United States to answer that question. When you read today's passage from Hosea, what he speaks still applies today and undoubtedly resonates with us.

The passage begins with a declaration: "Hear the word of the Lord, you children of Israel, for the Lord brings a charge against the inhabitants of the land" (Hosea 4:1). In the context of this legal language, God is the plaintiff and Israel is the defendant. The Lord is about to present His case against His people, detailing their offenses.

God laid out the initial charge: "There is no truth or mercy or knowledge of God in the land" (Hosea 4:1). This statement speaks to the source of the problem: a lack of knowledge of God, from which flows truth and mercy.

In many ways, we find ourselves in a similar situation. Consider the prevalence of moral relativism in our nation. When God's eternal, objective truths are replaced with subjective opinions or feelings, we see a disintegration of previously accepted societal norms. As we "break all restraint," the fabric of society begins to tear, leaving us vulnerable to the destructive behaviors that Hosea warns about: "swearing and lying, killing and stealing and committing adultery...with bloodshed upon bloodshed" (Hosea 4:2).

The Lord said of the Israelites, "My people are destroyed for lack of knowledge," and the reasons for both the lack of knowledge and the destruction were plentiful (Hosea 4:6).

Those who were commanded to teach the people about God had failed in their duties. Malachi 2:7 speaks to the responsibilities of priests: "For the lips of a priest should keep knowledge, and people should seek the law from his mouth; for he is the messenger of the Lord of hosts." Yet they forsook this obligation: "Her priests have violated My law and profaned My holy things; they have not distinguished between the holy and unholy, nor have they made known the difference between the unclean and the clean; and they have hidden their eyes from My Sabbaths, so that I am profaned among them" (Ezekiel 22:26). Therefore, God declared of them: "Because you have rejected knowledge, I also will reject you from being priest for Me" (Hosea 4:6).

Parents were to instruct their children to love the Lord and His law, as detailed in Psalm 78:5–7: "For He established a testimony in Jacob, and appointed a law in Israel, which He commanded our fathers, that they should make them known to their children; that the generation to come might know them, the children who would be born, that they may arise and declare them to their children, that they may set their hope in God, and not forget the works of God, but keep His commandments." Yet they, too, had forsaken this duty, as evidenced by their sentence: "Because you have forgotten the law of your God, I also will forget your children" (Hosea 4:6).

That pronouncement is a sobering reminder that our decisions, actions, and inaction can have a detrimental effect on future generations. In the same way that allowing our children to eat ice cream for every meal would deprive their physical bodies of essential nutrients, allowing them to consume the world's values and beliefs deprives their minds and spirits of God's essential truths. We adults must not falter in teaching our children to fear and love the Lord. We must lead them on paths of righteousness, daily reminding them of their baptismal identity in Christ.

The Israelites caused their own demise, reflecting what David wrote in one of his psalms: "The fool has said in his heart, 'There is no God.' They are corrupt, they have done abominable works, there is none who does good. The Lord looks down from heaven upon the children of men, to see if there are any who understand, who seek God. They have all turned aside, they have together become corrupt; there is none who does good, no, not one" (Psalm 14:1–3). The people were destroyed not only from without, when they were attacked by foreign nations and taken captive, but most thoroughly from within, when they lost their reverence for and obedience to God and His law.

It's impossible not to see the parallels between the charges and punishments the Lord brought against the Israelites and the condition of our nation today. When you reflect on the way our society once acknowledged biblical teachings, and see how we've become increasingly estranged from them, it can be easy to become discouraged.

However, each one of us can play a vital role in countering this tide of godlessness, beginning with ourselves. In humility and repentance, we can do as Solomon implored in Proverbs: "Incline your ear to wisdom, and apply your heart to understanding...if you seek her as silver, and search for her as for hidden treasures; then you will understand the fear of the Lord, and find the knowledge of God. For the Lord gives wisdom; from His mouth come knowledge and understanding" (Proverbs 2:2,

4–6). We can immerse ourselves in Scripture, allowing His Word to renew our hearts and minds, so we "may prove what is that good and acceptable and perfect will of God" (Romans 12:2).

We can impart God's wisdom to the next generation, ensuring that we "bring them up in the training and admonition of the Lord" (Ephesians 6:4).

And we can exemplify God's love, mercy, and truth, most importantly by sharing the Gospel of Jesus Christ, the light of the world—the beacon of hope in a dark world.

Prayer

Heavenly Father, we're often grieved by the state of our world. We confess that at times we've been complacent in a culture that denies Your truth. Please forgive us for the times we've forsaken Your knowledge. Help us be zealous in pursuing You, allowing us to be wise stewards of Your truth and raising up a generation that walks in righteousness. In the name of Jesus Christ, who reigns with You and the Holy Spirit, one God now and forever. Amen.

For Further Reflection

- Why do you think our nation has experienced a lack of the knowledge of God?
- Has there ever been a time when you allowed God's truth to be disparaged? How might you handle a similar situation in the future?

____

____

____

____

The nation You have blest
May well Your love declare,
From foes and fears at rest,
Protected by Your care.
For this bright day,
For this fair land—
Gifts of Your hand—
Our thanks we pay.

“Before You, Lord, We Bow”

Government as God's Ministers to Us

Let every soul be subject to the governing authorities. For there is no authority except from God, and the authorities that exist are appointed by God. Therefore whoever resists the authority resists the ordinance of God, and those who resist will bring judgment on themselves. For rulers are not a terror to good works, but to evil. Do you want to be unafraid of the authority? Do what is good, and you will have praise from the same. For he is God's minister to you for good. But if you do evil, be afraid; for he does not bear the sword in vain; for he is God's minister, an avenger to execute wrath on him who practices evil. Therefore you must be subject, not only because of wrath but also for conscience' sake. For because of this you also pay taxes, for they are God's ministers attending continually to this very thing. Render therefore to all their due: taxes to whom taxes are due, customs to whom customs, fear to whom fear, honor to whom honor.

—ROMANS 13:1–7

Scripture tells us that we're all created with the natural law: "For when Gentiles, who do not have the law, by nature do the things in the law, these, although not having the law, are a law to themselves, who show the work of the law written in their hearts, their conscience also bearing witness" (Romans

2:14–15). Our original parents, Adam and Eve, were the first to receive the gracious gift of God's law written on their hearts. Yet they chose to disobey and do the one thing they'd been commanded *not* to do: "And the Lord God commanded the man, saying, 'Of every tree of the garden you may freely eat; but of the tree of the knowledge of good and evil you shall not eat, for in the day that you eat of it you shall surely die'" (Genesis 2:16–17). Even though Adam and Eve ate of the fruit, the natural law remained on their hearts, but sin obscured it. So it remains to this day.

Government, or some type of earthly authority, is needed because of man's sinfulness. God's law, as epitomized in the Ten Commandments, shows us our sin, which Paul wrote about in Romans 7:7: "What shall we say then? Is the law sin? Certainly not! On the contrary, I would not have known sin except through the law. For I would not have known covetousness unless the law had said, 'You shall not covet'" (cf. Romans 3:20).

We're blessed that in our nation's laws we see evidence of God's law. Our laws protect private property, free speech, freedom of religion, and many other rights. Crimes like murder, rape, child abuse, theft, and other illegal activities lead to punishment, even if we disagree as to the type or duration of these punishments. Nevertheless, some of our laws—such as unfettered divorce or the legalization of abortion and euthanasia—also reflect the prevalence of sin.

Government, like any good gift the Lord gives us, can be used for evil. Whether it's tyrannical dictators who oppress and persecute their people, corrupt court systems that thwart justice, or individual lawmakers who financially enrich themselves at the expense of those they're intended to serve, history shows how mankind has and continues to corrupt the blessing of government.

In these situations, what's a proper Christian response? In what ways is it acceptable for us to resist the authorities?

We can look to both the Old Testament and New Testament for stories of faithful believers who withstood authorities' commands and chose to "obey God rather than men" (Acts 5:29).

One of the earliest examples is in Exodus 1:16, when Pharaoh demanded that the Hebrew midwives, Shiphrah and Puah, kill all of the male Hebrew children: "When you do the duties of a midwife for the Hebrew women, and see them on the birthstools, if it is a son, then you shall kill him; but if it is a daughter, then she shall live." Thankfully, these brave women defied Pharaoh's evil order and "saved the male children alive" (Exodus 1:17).

When Pharaoh summoned Shiphrah and Puah and asked them why they'd saved the male children, they replied, "Because the Hebrew women are not like the Egyptian women; for they are lively and give birth before the midwives come to them" (Exodus 1:19). Although we're not told whether this was a full truth or a half truth, what we do know is that the Lord approved of their actions, if not their explanation: "Therefore God dealt well with the midwives, and the people multiplied and grew very mighty. And so it was, because the midwives feared God, that He provided households for them" (Exodus 1:20–21). Since they chose to obey God rather than man, the Lord blessed them with families of their own.

In the New Testament, especially in the book of Acts, we find numerous instances of the apostles disobeying the commands of both the civil and religious leaders. When Peter, John, James, and Paul were directed to stop preaching in Jesus's name, they refused to do so, resulting in multiple imprisonments and beatings, and eventual martyrdom.

Paul, when he was arrested for preaching the Gospel in Jerusalem, leveraged his Roman citizenship to prevent himself from being unlawfully scourged and interrogated (Acts 22:22–29). Later on, when he was arrested at Caesarea, he once again used his status as a Roman citizen to appeal to Caesar (Acts 25:10–12). God used Paul's shrewd tactics to further the Gospel, as each of these instances gave the apostle opportunities to share his testimony with different audiences, including powerful, influential rulers.

In comparison to the righteous resistance of these believers, we have an example of the One who perfectly obeyed the authorities, Jesus Christ. Although He establishes all earthly authorities, He willingly submitted to them—even when they unjustly accused and persecuted Him.

When Jesus was brought before Pontius Pilate, Pilate asked Jesus where He was from but received no answer. "Then Pilate said to Him, 'Are You not speaking to me? Do You not know that I have power to crucify You, and power to release You?'" (John 19:10).

Jesus did respond to this question, saying, "You could have no power at all against Me unless it had been given you from above" (John 19:11). He informed Pilate that he didn't come to his position because of his own talent or intelligence. God had put Pilate in place so that the world might be saved through Christ's crucifixion.

Jesus's allegiance was to the Father, and while in the Garden of Gethsemane, He'd prayed, "Father, if it is Your will, take this cup away from Me; nevertheless not My will, but Yours, be done" (Luke 22:42). If submitting to the Father also meant submitting to the earthly authorities' plan to execute Him, Jesus would obey. Jesus Christ, "who, being in the form of God, did not consider it robbery to be equal with God, but made Himself of no reputation, taking the form of a bondservant, and coming in the likeness of men. And being found in appearance as a man, He humbled Himself and became obedient to the point of death, even the death of the cross" (Philippians 2:6–8).

Whether we're resisting or obeying civil authorities, our actions must reflect God's love, mercy, and truth, doing as Jesus commanded: "Let your light so shine before men, that they may see your good works and glorify your Father in heaven" (Matthew 5:16).

Prayer

Lord Almighty, help us to honor the authorities You have placed over us, and allow us to be citizens who love You and our neighbor. Grant us discernment to know when we must resist something that our government demands of us, as well as the courage to stand firm in faith in obedience to You. And if we must resist, may we do so in a way that reflects Your wisdom and love. In Jesus's holy name we pray. Amen.

For Further Reflection

- What do you think it means when Paul says that civil authorities don't "bear the sword in vain"?
- If you're ever in a position where you must resist an authority God has placed over you, what steps can you take to ensure that this resistance is rooted in truth, justice, and love, and not in rebellion?

Trusting God Amid War

The nations raged, the kingdoms were moved;
He uttered His voice, the earth melted.
The Lord of hosts is with us;
The God of Jacob is our refuge. Selah
Come, behold the works of the Lord,
Who has made desolations in the earth.
He makes wars cease to the end of the earth;
He breaks the bow and cuts the spear in two;
He burns the chariot in the fire.
Be still, and know that I am God;
I will be exalted among the nations,
I will be exalted in the earth!

—PSALM 46:6–10

As I mentioned in the book's introduction, my adopted dad was in the army, although he was retired by the time I was born. I was raised to respect and appreciate our soldiers and to be grateful for all they'd sacrificed to serve the United States and keep us safe. I love seeing the American flag on display and witnessing military flyovers at events. And hearing "Taps" played on a lone bugle always moves me to tears.

It had never occurred to me that some people believe it's impossible for Christians to be soldiers because they shouldn't engage in violence, or they might be forced to act against their beliefs and values. However, as in any other civil role, Christians who are enlisted in the military can reflect God's honor, as well as protect the vulnerable and uphold justice, in both times of war and times of peace. The Lord calls some to be peacemakers and some to be protectors, and He can use both to serve His purposes.

The Old Testament contains numerous stories of battles and wars. The psalms, in particular, discuss war a lot—which makes sense, since David wrote many of these songs, and he was a man of war. He desired to build a temple for the Lord in Jerusalem, but as he explained to Solomon, "The word of the Lord came to me, saying, 'You have shed much blood and have made great wars; you shall not build a house for My name, because you have shed much blood on the earth in My sight'" (1 Chronicles 22:8). As Israel's king and military leader for forty years, David was intimately familiar with all that war entailed.

Although David didn't write Psalm 46, it contains many similar ideas to what he expressed in his inspired writings, such as God's sovereignty over all creation, His protection of His people, and the truth that salvation is found only in Him.

Today's excerpt begins with the words "The nations raged, the kingdoms were moved" (Psalm 46:6). In a sinful world, human conflict is inevitable. Though people often talk about establishing "peace on earth," that reality is impossible with mankind in its current state, as even Christians are both saints and sinners in the present age.

However, the phrase "the kingdoms were moved" reflects the truth that nations don't rise and fall of their own volition. As it says in Psalm 44:2–3, "You drove out the nations with Your hand, but them You planted; you afflicted the peoples, and cast them out. For they did not gain possession of the land by their own sword, nor did their own arm save them; but it was Your right hand, Your arm, and the light of Your countenance, because You favored them."

When the Israelites entered the Promised Land, their victories weren't due to their own might or brilliant military strategies. The Israelites prevailed because the Lord went before them and was with them. As Moses told Joshua when anointing him the new leader of Israel: "The Lord will give them over to you, that you may do to them according to every commandment which I have commanded you.... And the Lord, He is the One who goes before you. He will be with you, He will not leave you nor forsake you; do not fear nor be dismayed" (Deuteronomy 31:5, 8).

The Lord's sovereignty is also reflected in the second part of verse 6 in Psalm 46: "He uttered His voice, the earth melted." God's voice can create, and it also can destroy. Yet only He has the ultimate power of creation and destruction, as He says in Isaiah 45:7: "I form the light and create darkness, I make peace and create calamity; I, the Lord, do all these things."

Verse 7 of the psalm refers to God as "the Lord of hosts." He's the commander in chief of the heavenly armies that battle His enemies and ours. On the eve of Joshua's defeat of Jericho, a man appeared before him. When he asked the man whether He was for or against the Israelites, the man answered, "No, but as Commander of the army of the Lord I have now come" (Joshua 5:14). Whether for or against the temporal endeavors of nations, God is always on the eternal side of the faithful, and "if God is for us, who can be against us?" (Romans 8:31).

In verse 8 of the psalm, we read that the Lord "has made desolations in the earth," but that He also "makes wars cease to the end of the earth; He breaks the bow and cuts the spear in two; He burns the chariot in the fire" (Psalm 46:9). Neither our weapons nor our treaties determine peace—only God does this. The United States has formidable military capabilities. However, "no king is saved by the multitude of an army; a mighty man is not delivered by great strength. A horse is a vain hope for safety; neither shall it deliver any by its great strength.... Our soul waits for the Lord; He is our help and our shield" (Psalm 33:16–17, 20).

That judgment precedes peace can be seen in the death and resurrection of Jesus Christ: "But God demonstrates His own love toward us, in that while we were still sinners, Christ died for us. Much more then, having now been justified by His blood, we shall be saved from wrath through Him. For if when we were enemies we were reconciled to God through the death of His Son, much more, having been reconciled, we shall be saved by His life" (Romans 5:8–10).

The eternal battle—against sin, death, and the devil—was already won by an army of one: the Lamb of God who died on the cross to take away the sins of the world. In Him, we can be still, for He gives us rest and peace (Matthew 11:28; John 14:27). And in Him we know God (John 14:9).

Temporal and spiritual warfare will continue until Christ returns, and when He does, "[He] will be exalted among the nations, [He] will be exalted in the earth" (Psalm 46:10).

Until then, may He protect our nation from violent conflicts, and may He strengthen and preserve everyone who serves in our military.

Prayer

Mighty Lord, You have fought many battles for Your people, and we know that even when the violence and chaos of war seems to abound across the globe, You are in control. Help us to remember that our ultimate hope isn't anchored in governments or armies, but in Your faithfulness and the peace we have with You and with one another in Christ Jesus. In His name we pray. Amen.

For Further Reflection

- Do you think it's acceptable for Christians to serve in the military? Why or why not?
- How should Christians respond when the United States is involved in military conflicts that appear to be unjust?

Protecting the Least of These

Then He said to the disciples, "It is impossible that no offenses should come, but woe to him through whom they do come! It would be better for him if a millstone were hung around his neck, and he were thrown into the sea, than that he should offend one of these little ones."

—LUKE 17:1–2

There's a saying that you can tell a lot about a society based on the way it treats its youngest and oldest members.

If that's true, then the United States has a massive problem, because some of the greatest evils of our time are perpetrated against children: abortion, infanticide, molestation, child abuse, child pornography, child trafficking, a push for the acceptance of pedophilia, the administration of hormone blockers and gender transitioning procedures... Even typing that list makes my stomach churn as I think of the millions of children being hurt, body and soul, each and every day in our country.

As someone who has personally suffered some of these evils, and as the mother of two children, these aren't the kinds of issues I'm willing to stay silent on.

In today's passage from Luke, Jesus makes it abundantly clear that severe judgment befalls those who lead children astray or harm them in any way. His words convey the sanctity and purity of childhood and the accountability we have to protect the youngest and most vulnerable in our nation.

That protection should begin at the moment of conception. The psalmist wrote, "For You formed my inward parts; You covered me in my mother's womb. I will praise You, for I am fearfully and wonderfully made; marvelous are Your works, and that my soul knows very well. My frame was not hidden from You, when I was made in secret, and skillfully wrought in the lowest parts of the earth. Your eyes saw my substance, being yet unformed. And in Your book they all were written, the days fashioned for me, when as yet there were none of them" (Psalm 139:13–16).

These verses portray a beautiful and profound truth: Even before conception, the Lord knows us and has our entire life story written in His Book. And from conception onward, He knits us together in our mother's womb, showing the care and intentionality with which the Lord creates every child. This knowledge should compel us to protect something so unique and valuable.

The amazing capacity of unborn children is shown in the Gospel of Luke, when Mary, who was pregnant with Jesus, visited her cousin Elizabeth, who was pregnant with John the Baptist. Mary arrived and greeted her cousin, and "the babe leaped in her womb; and Elizabeth was filled with the Holy Spirit" (Luke 1:41). Elizabeth then exclaimed: "Blessed are you among women, and blessed is the fruit of your womb! But why is this granted to me, that the mother of my Lord should come to me? For indeed, as soon as the voice of your greeting sounded in my ears, the babe leaped in my womb for joy. Blessed is she who believed, for there will be a fulfillment of those things which were told her from the Lord" (Luke 1:42–45; cf. Luke 1:15).

Even as a fetus, John the Baptist was able to experience joy, as the one who would "make straight the way of the Lord" celebrated the arrival of the One he'd later declare "the Lamb of God who takes away the sin of the world" (John 1:23, 29).

Unborn children were also deemed fully human in the Mosaic law: "If men fight, and hurt a woman with child, so that she gives birth prematurely, yet no harm follows, he shall surely be punished accordingly as the woman's husband imposes on him; and he shall pay as the judges determine. But if any harm follows, then you shall give life for life, eye for eye, tooth for tooth, hand for hand, foot for foot" (Exodus 21:22–24). If men, who'd been tasked with protecting life since God created Adam, allowed their anger and violence to hurt or kill an unborn child, their punishment was to be commensurate with the harm they caused—and if the child died, then their lives were forfeit. This law serves to remind us of the high value the Lord places on all life, including unborn children.

The law provided comparable punishment for kidnapping: "He who kidnaps a man and sells him, or if he is found in his hand, shall surely be put to death" (Exodus 21:16). Child trafficking falls under the category of kidnapping, since it takes a child from his or her parents, whether under false pretenses or brazenly snatching them away, for sexual abuse or forced labor. As with causing harm to an unborn child, the punishment for such an act was death.

Although many offenses toward children are physical in nature, the mental and emotional harm of these acts can't be denied. Mental and emotional harm can be brought about in other ways too. This notion is expressed in Song of Solomon 2:7: "I charge you, O daughters of Jerusalem, by the gazelles or by the does of the field, do not stir up nor awaken love until it pleases." Exposure to pornography and other sexualized content, which many children have access to through internet-connected devices, can set the stage for a lifetime of dysfunctional behavior and addiction. These days, even preschool-aged children are exposed to sexual education materials and ideas such as gender theory that are completely inappropriate—not only from a moral or religious perspective but also from a developmental perspective.

When my husband and I were considering where our children should be educated, I was on the fence about private school. But when I researched the school's mission and vision, one word resonated deeply with me: *virtue*. The school has a commitment to preserving children's innocence and shielding them from harmful influences, including those of a sexual nature. The school agrees that such teachings and conversations are rightly conducted between parents and their own children. And while these discussions can be hard, we owe it to our children to ensure they're being taught about sexuality according to God's design in the one-flesh union of husband and wife.

Psalm 127:3 says, "Behold, children are a heritage from the Lord, the fruit of the womb is a reward." May the words of Proverbs 31:8–9 serve as our call to action to advocate for the safety and well-being of these little ones, for they are indeed a heritage from the Lord: "Open your mouth for the speechless, in the cause of all who are appointed to die. Open your mouth, judge righteously, and plead the cause of the poor and needy."

Prayer

Lord Jesus Christ, when Your disciples rebuked those who brought little children to You, You said, "Let the little children come to Me, and do not forbid them; for of such is the kingdom of God" (Mark 10:14). Then You "took them up in [Your] arms, laid [Your] hands on them, and blessed them" (Mark 10:16). May You shield every child in our country from harm and grant us the courage to advocate for them even from conception. In Your name we pray. Amen.

For Further Reflection

- What are the results of America's general lack of protecting our nation's children?
- How can you advocate for the children in your community?

____

____

____

____

____

____

The Lord Appoints

Do not say,
"Why were the former days better than these?"
For you do not inquire wisely concerning this....
In the day of prosperity be joyful,
But in the day of adversity consider:
Surely God has appointed the one as well as the other,
So that man can find out nothing that will come after him.

—ECCLESIASTES 7:10, 14

A*h, the good old days...*

Do you ever find yourself reflecting on years or decades past, reminiscing about how much better things used to be?

Modern life can be exhausting in every way—mentally, emotionally, physically, and spiritually. We're exposed to more information than our brains can absorb and process. News, social media, and other outlets stir up our anger, frustration, and sadness. Our sedentary lifestyles and dietary choices can leave us feeling tired and lethargic. And the world tempts us to forsake worship of the Lord.

When the present feels overwhelming or deficient, it can be easy to think: *If only things could go back to the way they were.*

We might romanticize the past, feeling that life was simpler or more fulfilling in some way—especially in regard to the state of America.

However, in this passage from Ecclesiastes, Solomon warns against such a mindset.

Biblical scholars believe that Solomon wrote Ecclesiastes toward the end of his reign as king over Israel. Under his rule, the nation had experienced unprecedented peace and prosperity. And Solomon himself was sought out by people like the queen of Sheba to bask in his God-given wisdom and see his vast wealth for themselves.

Early in his reign, the Lord spoke to Solomon, telling him that He'd bless him, provided the king continued to love and serve Him only. But as we read in 1 Kings and 2 Chronicles, Solomon's pagan wives led his heart astray, and he forsook his fellowship with God in favor of man-made idols.

When you read the whole book of Ecclesiastes, there seems to be little to no trace of the godly man who proclaimed the Lord's glory at the dedication of the temple in Jerusalem, who implored the Israelites to "let your heart therefore be loyal to the Lord our God, to walk in His statutes and keep His commandments, as at this day" (1 Kings 8:61). Instead, we find a jaded ruler who has spent his life and riches pursuing every pleasure known to man, yet found all of it lacking: "I have seen all the works that are done under the sun; and indeed, all is vanity and grasping for the wind" (Ecclesiastes 1:14).

Solomon's life had started off blessed in every way imaginable, but even he felt that longing for the past was foolish.

The reasons any of us long for the past vary. Maybe we miss family and friends who have died. Perhaps we're divorced and mourn for our broken marriage. It could be that we're estranged from our adult children and wish for the days when we were close to them. We miss our days of youthful vitality.

When these thoughts and feelings emerge within us, what's really going on?

Regardless of what's motivating us, the same holds true in every instance: We're longing for the past because we want to avoid dealing with something unpleasant in the present.

We don't want to miss people who've died because this makes us sad. We don't want to be divorced because single parenting is hard. We don't want to navigate messy relationships with our adult children. We don't want to feel the aches and pains of living with an aging body.

As Solomon rightly points out, life isn't on a perfectly smooth continuum. In Ecclesiastes 7:13 he asks, "Consider the work of God; for who can make straight what He has made crooked?" Oh, life definitely gets crooked! However, this verse asserts an important truth: Whether our current path through life is straight or crooked, it's the work of God. This truth is also stated in Ecclesiastes 7:14, where Solomon says that the Lord appoints both prosperity and adversity. We can take tremendous comfort knowing that no matter what our path looks like, as an individual or as a nation, "To everything there is a season, a time for every purpose under heaven" (Ecclesiastes 3:1).

God can take any and every adversity we face and transform it into something beneficial.

One of the clearest examples of this is Joseph, whose story can be found in Genesis 37 through 50.

Joseph was the favored son of Jacob, one of the Bible's patriarchs. Jacob's ten older sons became so jealous of their younger brother that they sold him into slavery. Joseph ended up in Egypt, where Potiphar, one of Pharaoh's officials, purchased him. All was well until Potiphar's wife falsely accused Joseph of assaulting her, at which point the young Hebrew was thrown into prison. He languished there until Pharaoh had troubling nightmares that none of his magicians or wise men could interpret. Joseph was summoned to tell Pharaoh what the dreams meant—a gift Joseph rightly informed Pharaoh was from the Lord. Pharaoh then elevated Joseph to second-in-command over all Egypt. In addition to this reversal of fortunes, Joseph was blessed with a wife and two sons.

When a famine that had been warned about in Pharaoh's dreams came to pass, Jacob sent his ten older sons to Egypt to buy grain. At first, Joseph didn't reveal his identity to his brothers. But after some drama and intrigue, he did, and invited all of his brothers and their families, as well as his father, Jacob, to live in Egypt.

You'd struggle to find someone whose life's peaks and valleys were more extreme than Joseph's. At any point, you could understand if he yearned for the past—whether the carefree days of his youth in Jacob's house or his years of prestige in Potiphar's house. But throughout the ordeal, the Bible gives no indication that he complained or had a "woe is me" attitude. So what did he make of all that he'd endured?

After Jacob died, Joseph's older brothers worried that he'd exact revenge on them. They bowed down before him, essentially throwing themselves on his mercy. In response, Joseph told them, "Do not be afraid, for am I in the place of God? But as for you, you meant evil against me; but God meant it for good, in order to bring it about as it is this day, to save many people alive" (Genesis 50:19–20).

Joseph epitomizes being joyful in prosperity and recognizing the Lord's will being done through adversity.

When we dwell on the past, whether the positive or the negative, we run the risk of missing the extraordinary and meaningful moments right in front of our eyes. Let's give thanks and praise to the Lord for the innumerable blessings we have in our life and in our nation. Even when things get "crooked," we can have complete confidence that it's the work of His hands.

Prayer

Lord, Your thoughts are not our thoughts, and Your ways are not our ways (Isaiah 55:8). We repent of the times we've longed for the past to the detriment of the present, losing our focus on the blessings You've given us today. Please help us embrace our current season, whether it's full of prosperity or adversity, trusting that You have a purpose for every moment. We ask this in Jesus's precious and holy name. Amen.

For Further Reflection

- What aspects of the past do you find yourself longing for? Make a list of these items and then create a list of all you're grateful for in the present. Does focusing on your present blessings change your feelings about the past in any way?
- When faced with adversity, what is the first thing you do? Do you complain about the problem, blame someone or something else, or try to avoid the problem altogether? Do you try to learn from the experience? Do you implore God for understanding? Regardless of how you typically respond, consider ways you can make going to the Lord the first thing you do.

No danger, thirst, or hunger,
No pain or poverty,
No earthly tyrant's anger
Shall ever vanquish me.
Though earth should break asunder,
My fortress You shall be;
No fire or sword or thunder
Shall sever You from me.

"If God Himself Be for Me"

To Live in Quiet and Peace

Therefore I exhort first of all that supplications, prayers, intercessions, and giving of thanks be made for all men, for kings and all who are in authority, that we may lead a quiet and peaceable life in all godliness and reverence. For this is good and acceptable in the sight of God our Savior, who desires all men to be saved and to come to the knowledge of the truth.

—1 TIMOTHY 2:1–4

We're extremely blessed to live in a country where we can vote for those in public office. From the local councilmember to the mayor to the governor, all the way up to the president, we can stand in that voting booth and select the people we feel most closely align with our Christian values and beliefs and are best qualified for the position. Although voting isn't mandatory, it's something we shouldn't take for granted. Many people around the world don't have this opportunity and freedom.

Neither did the Apostle Paul. Although he was a Roman citizen, he didn't get to vote for any of his local or national political leaders, because they were appointed. The citizens had no say in the matter, regardless of how corrupt those individuals were.

This is especially significant in the context of Paul's first letter to Timothy, the young pastor whom Paul mentored and considered his spiritual son, referring to him as "a true son in the faith" (1 Timothy 1:2). In the middle of the first century, the notoriously wicked Nero became emperor of Rome. His rule was marked by tyranny and violence, particularly against Christians. He blamed the Great Fire of Rome on the Christians, using this as an excuse to enact state-sponsored persecution. Believers were arrested in droves and subjected to torture and excruciating deaths, including being set on fire or crucified.

Against such a backdrop, it's even more remarkable that Paul specifically exhorts Timothy to encourage the believers of the Ephesian church, where Timothy served as bishop, to pray for their leaders: "Therefore I exhort first of all that supplications, prayers, intercessions, and giving of thanks be made for all men, for kings and all who are in authority" (1 Timothy 2:1–2).

In using multiple words to describe these petitions, Paul communicated the idea that there isn't simply one "type" of prayer. You can think of the terms this way: A supplication is something we ask for. Prayer is a more general term, for speaking to God as a Father. Intercessions are offered on the behalf of others. And thanksgiving is just what it sounds like: expressing gratitude to God.

When we pray to the Lord, we can use all of these approaches. And we're to offer them "for all men, for kings and all who are in authority" (1 Timothy 2:1–2). Even for an evil emperor like Nero? Yes. For tax collectors who confiscate more of the people's wealth than they ought? Yes. For authorities who abuse their privileged positions? Yes. Paul's language couldn't be clearer: *for all men.*

Of course, it goes against our sinful flesh to pray for our enemies. Yet we Christians have a humbling and profound responsibility to pray not only for ourselves and those we care about but also for our enemies, as Christ Himself exhorts in Luke 6:27–28: "But I say to you who hear: Love your enemies, do good to those who hate you, bless those who curse you, and pray for those who spitefully use you." On the cross, He Himself modeled this lavish grace and mercy, when He implored, "Father, forgive them, for they do not know what they do" (Luke 23:34).

We can't underestimate the power our prayers have for our leaders, who daily make decisions that impact our families, our churches, our communities, our nation, and our world. Every day, we can ask God to grant them wisdom and a heart that aligns with His will.

Even more so, Paul said that we should pray for leaders unto a specific end: "that we may lead a quiet and peaceable life in all godliness and reverence" (1 Timothy 2:2). How could that not have been a deep desire of the apostle, as he watched his fellow brothers and sisters in Christ be imprisoned and martyred for their beliefs?

When our leaders rule with integrity, when the rule of law is followed, and when justice is being properly applied, social peace can flourish. The ultimate purpose of a peaceful society is God's purpose: that the church can fulfill the Great Commission Jesus gave in Matthew 28:19–20: "Go therefore and make disciples of all the nations, baptizing them in the name of the

Father and of the Son and of the Holy Spirit, teaching them to observe all things that I have commanded you."

Paul reinforced this truth when he wrote that the goal of his guidance was to ensure that the Gospel could be preached without hindrance, because the Lord "desires all men to be saved and to come to the knowledge of the truth" (1 Timothy 2:4).

Unlike Paul, Timothy, and other early Christians, we're blessed to live in a nation where we have an unfettered ability to believe in and worship the Lord and share the Gospel. Granted, we might encounter opposition to these endeavors from civil authorities, but the freedom of religion is enshrined in the Constitution of the United States. Nevertheless, we shouldn't take this freedom for granted and should be willing to stand up against any authority that would deprive us of this right.

Our nation struggles with political turmoil, social unrest, and moral confusion. We might get frustrated with those who lead us, wondering why they don't "fix" all of these problems. Yet Paul's exhortation encourages us to pivot from criticism and complaint to supplication and gratitude, asking God to intervene for all people and for the good of the Gospel of Jesus Christ.

Prayer

Heavenly Father, we thank and praise You that we live in a nation where we may worship You freely and share the truth of Jesus Christ—His life, death, and resurrection—with all. May we never take this freedom for granted, and may we pray for our leaders to enact and enforce laws and policies that allow us to live quiet and peaceable lives, so we may pursue those good works You've prepared in advance for us to do (Ephesians 2:10). In Christ's name we pray. Amen.

For Further Reflection

- Do you see any ways that a lack of "a quiet and peaceable life" for American citizens has hindered our ability to worship or share the Gospel?
- In what ways do you see society and the church flourish when we have peace in our nation?

Pulling Down and Building Up

The instant I speak concerning a nation and concerning a kingdom, to pluck up, to pull down, and to destroy it, if that nation against whom I have spoken turns from its evil, I will relent of the disaster that I thought to bring upon it. And the instant I speak concerning a nation and concerning a kingdom, to build and to plant it, if it does evil in My sight so that it does not obey My voice, then I will relent concerning the good with which I said I would benefit it. Now therefore, speak to the men of Judah and to the inhabitants of Jerusalem, saying, "Thus says the Lord: 'Behold, I am fashioning a disaster and devising a plan against you. Return now every one from his evil way, and make your ways and your doings good.'"

—JEREMIAH 18:7–11

Have you ever seen anyone work a potter's wheel, or have you ever worked one yourself? It looks like a lot of fun, but I suspect that it's harder than it looks.

You have to center the clay on the wheel at all times, or else your finished product will be lopsided. You must keep the clay at the ideal moisture, so it doesn't crumble or liquefy. If you spin the wheel too fast or too slow, it will be hard to mold the clay into the desired shape. Your foot, hands, and eyes must work together in perfect harmony to achieve pottery perfection.

Prior to the verses in today's reading, the Lord called to the prophet Jeremiah and told him, "Arise and go down to the potter's house, and there I will cause you to hear My words" (Jeremiah 18:2). Jeremiah did as the Lord commanded and found the potter working at his wheel: "And the vessel that he made of clay was marred in the hand of the potter; so he made it again into another vessel, as it seemed good to the potter to make" (Jeremiah 18:4). The Lord then used the potter as a metaphor of His own creative work: "'O house of Israel, can I not do with you as this potter?' says the Lord. 'Look, as the clay is in the potter's hand, so are you in My hand, O house of Israel!'" (Jeremiah 18:6).

Depending on your status before God, to be in His hand can be either a source of terror or a source of comfort. For the unrepentant sinner, to be in the Lord's hands is to face His judgment and wrath. For the repentant sinner saved by grace through faith, to be in the Lord's hands is a place of peace and security. We saints are blessed to be those whom Paul describes as "the vessels of mercy, which He had prepared beforehand for glory" (Romans 9:23).

During Jeremiah's ministry, the nation of Israel was hanging in the balance. Prophet after prophet had been sent to warn the Israelites of their impending doom if they didn't turn away from their sin and rebellion against the Lord. Sadly, they stayed on their path and were sent into exile in Babylon. As was said in Isaiah 45:9: "Woe to him who strives with his Maker! Let the potsherd strive with the potsherds of the earth! Shall the clay say to him who forms it, 'What are you making?' Or shall your handiwork say, 'He has no hands'?"

The image of a potter shaping clay is a powerful, beautiful picture of God's active role in human history. He didn't just create the world, set it in motion, and leave us to our own devices. He is a hands-on God, present and moving not only in the lives of His children but also in the events of every nation on earth, including America. When we study history, particularly in the Bible, we can see how God orchestrated the rise and fall of many nations, including Egypt, Babylon, Assyria, Nineveh, and even that of His chosen people, Israel. Each of these nations was shaped and molded for the Lord's purposes, to accomplish His will and serve a greater purpose in His divine plan of salvation.

We can see this as we reflect on the way He orchestrated the birth of His Son, Jesus Christ, and the spread of the Gospel after Jesus's death and resurrection: born to minister in a nation on the Mediterranean Sea, a major hub of global travel and trade, and born to minister during the Roman Empire, a time of general peace. In many other ways, the evidence of the Lord's hands perfectly shaping all circumstances to benefit the early church reminds us of how involved and intentional He is in human affairs. We can take great hope in this knowledge. If He can order such grand, sweeping events throughout millennia, surely He can order our days aright too.

Although the Lord is loving and merciful, He's also holy and just. He cannot tolerate sin, and therefore must punish it. If a nation turns away from Him, consequences will follow. We've already seen some consequences in the United States. A lack of respect for His design has led to divorce, broken families, and abortion. A covetousness for material possessions has led to a lack of appreciation for the Lord's provision. These and many other ills plague our society.

Yet even today, the Lord is willing to forgive and restore: "If that nation against whom I have spoken turns from its evil, I will relent of the disaster that I thought to bring upon it" (Jeremiah 18:8).

If the nation will seek Him first, it can experience His grace and favor.

Prayer

Lord Almighty, Isaiah 64:8 says, "You are our Father; we are the clay, and You our potter; and all we are the work of Your hand." But sometimes we feel like broken potsherds, and the world around us feels like a messy pile of broken pottery. So we pray for our country, that we will obey Your voice and turn from evil, and make our ways and doings good. We trust in Your divine will, knowing that we are safely in Your hand. Amen.

For Further Reflection

- Does knowing that you're in the Lord's hands make you fearful or joyful? Why?
- When you consider that the Lord pulls down and builds up nations, how does this truth affect your understanding of history?

____

____

____

____

____

The Power of Intercessory Prayer

Then I set my face toward the Lord God to make request by prayer and supplications, with fasting, sackcloth, and ashes. And I prayed to the Lord my God, and made confession, and said, "O Lord, great and awesome God, who keeps His covenant and mercy with those who love Him, and with those who keep His commandments, we have sinned and committed iniquity, we have done wickedly and rebelled, even by departing from Your precepts and Your judgments....
"O Lord, to us belongs shame of face, to our kings, our princes, and our fathers, because we have sinned against You. To the Lord our God belong mercy and forgiveness, though we have rebelled against Him."

—DANIEL 9:3–5, 8–9

Although Daniel is probably most famous for surviving his attempted execution in the lions' den, or maybe even for his ability to interpret dreams, the book of the Bible that bears his name illustrates one of his extraordinary, godly characteristics: He was a man of prayer.

Throughout the book of Daniel, we see him prostrating himself before God, confessing his individual sins and the sins of the nation, asking for forgiveness. At every opportunity, he magnifies the Lord, giving Him the credit for any blessing that occurs.

For instance, when King Nebuchadnezzar summons Daniel to explain the first dream recorded, part of the prophet's declaration includes words of humility: "I thank You and praise You, O God of my fathers; You have given me wisdom and might" (Daniel 2:23). Contrast this statement with King Nebuchadnezzar's prideful boast in Daniel 4:30.

After Belshazzar, Nebuchadnezzar's son who succeeded him, was slain, Darius the Mede became ruler. Under the new king's reign, the Lord blessed Daniel through Darius by appointing Daniel as governor and even "gave thought to setting him over the whole realm" (Daniel 6:3). This didn't sit well with the other governors. They knew that Daniel was well-esteemed, and said, "We shall not find any charge against this Daniel unless we find it against him concerning the law of his God" (Daniel 6:5).

Daniel had a reputation of the best sort: He was known as a faithful worshipper of Yahweh.

At this point, Daniel was about sixty years old, and he'd been taken into captivity as a young man (Daniel 5:31, 1:3–4, 6). We don't know how old he was when he was taken to Babylon, but even if he was only in his early twenties, he'd been residing in the kingdom for a few decades and had served with distinction under three kings.

From the onset of his captivity, Daniel and his companions set themselves apart, refusing to eat or drink from the king's table and insisting that even without that rich and delicious food, they'd remain healthy and vibrant. They made it clear that their first and foremost loyalty was to God. Daniel's three friends—Shadrach (Hananiah), Meshach (Mishael), and Abed-Nego

(Azariah)—had further demonstrated their faith in the Lord when they refused to fall down and worship the golden statue of King Nebuchadnezzar and were thrown into a fiery furnace.

Later, when Daniel's political enemies set a trap for him, they rightly acknowledged that the only "weak spot" he had was for the Lord. So they went before King Darius and said, "All the governors of the kingdom, the administrators and satraps, the counselors and advisors, have consulted together to establish a royal statute and to make a firm decree, that whoever petitions any god or man for thirty days, except you, O king, shall be cast into the den of lions" (Daniel 6:7). As noted in Daniel 6:8, once this was signed into law, it couldn't be altered.

How did Daniel respond to this new decree?

"Now when Daniel knew that the writing was signed, he went home. And in his upper room, with his windows open toward Jerusalem, he knelt down on his knees three times that day, and prayed and gave thanks before his God, as was his custom since early days" (Daniel 6:10).

Without any hesitation, he defied the king's law—not just once but three times, and completely out in the open.

His enemies "caught him in the act" and immediately reported this infraction to the king. Although Darius tried to find a loophole to save Daniel, he was unable to do so. Thus, the prophet was cast into the lions' den, from which the Lord delivered him: "My God sent His angel and shut the lions' mouths, so that they have not hurt me, because I was found innocent before Him; and also, O king, I have done no wrong before you" (Daniel 6:22).

The Lord had shown Himself mighty to save, and Daniel had seen that repeatedly in Babylon.

Therefore, when he comes before the Lord in prayer in chapter 9, he does so according to his custom. But this time, in addition to setting his face toward God, he prepared by fasting and donning sackcloth and ashes—the former a spiritual discipline and the latter a sign of contrition.

Daniel's entire prayer is included in Daniel 9:4–19. It begins with praising the Lord, acknowledging His magnificence and lauding His character. Admiration of His glory is folded into other portions of the prayer. Daniel then transitions into confession, specifically stating the sins of him and his people. After this, he makes his supplication to God, and finally closes with a heartfelt cry: "O Lord, hear! O Lord, forgive! O Lord, listen and act! Do not delay for Your own sake, my God, for Your city and Your people are called by Your name" (Daniel 9:19).

Reading this passage provides us with a beautiful model of what intercessory prayer for a nation can look like, especially the structure: adoration, confession, supplication.

But the story continued. Daniel "was speaking, praying, and confessing [his] sin and the sin of [his] people Israel, and presenting [his] supplication before the Lord [his] God" (Daniel 9:20). While he was praying, God sent the angel Gabriel to him. Along with providing insight for the prophet's vision, Gabriel told Daniel, "At the beginning of your supplications the command went out, and I have come to tell you, for you are greatly beloved" (Daniel 9:23).

The Lord chose to honor His prophet's request. One day soon, Cyrus, the king of Persia, would issue a decree allowing the Jews to return to their homeland and rebuild it, which we read about in the books of Ezra and Nehemiah. Although the Israelites had been unfaithful to the Lord, He remained faithful to them—as He remains faithful to us, "who are called according to His purpose" (Romans 8:28).

Just like Daniel, we can pray and intercede for our nation. As it says in 1 John 5:14–15, "Now this is the confidence that we have in Him, that if we ask anything according to His will, He hears us. And if we know that He hears us, whatever we ask, we know that we have the petitions that we have asked of Him." Let us go boldly before Him, glorifying Him, confessing our sins and the sins of our nation, and asking for His will to be done.

Prayer

Dear Lord, please grant us hearts like Your servant Daniel, fervently committed to praying to You daily. And when we petition You on behalf of our nation, may our prayers glorify You. Let us be contrite, acknowledging our sins and shortcomings. May we confidently present our petitions to You, knowing and trusting that You will hear and answer them according to Your perfect will. In Jesus's name we pray. Amen.

For Further Reflection

- Read Nehemiah 1:5–11, another example of intercessory prayer for a nation. In what ways is it similar to Daniel 9:4–19? In what ways does it differ?
- Select either Daniel or Nehemiah's prayer to use as a model intercessory prayer for the United States. After you pray, meditate on the experience of using Scripture as the basis for your prayers.

A Temple of the Holy Spirit

Or do you not know that your body is the temple of the Holy Spirit who is in you, whom you have from God, and you are not your own? For you were bought at a price; therefore glorify God in your body and in your spirit, which are God's.

—1 CORINTHIANS 6:19–20

The United States is one of the wealthiest nations in the world, yet it's also one of the unhealthiest—despite the fact that we have access to some of the best medical facilities in the world and spend more money on healthcare than any other country.

How did we get here?

Undoubtedly, there's plenty of blame to go around. The government hasn't always done the best job regulating what does or doesn't go into our food. Food manufacturers have prioritized profits over producing healthy products. Marketing teams work overtime to make foods and drinks seem appealing. Tired and overworked parents sometimes feed their children meals that are more convenient than nutritious.

All of these factors have played a role in getting us to where we are today. Yet we must not overlook where we should seek answers first and foremost: ourselves.

I grew up in a relatively poor household. We ate a lot of cheap, processed foods, so I developed an appetite for such things. However, once I was out of the home and on my own, I still continued to make poor food choices. Throughout my life, I've wrestled with this issue.

Over the past few years, I've discovered that it's not truly a food issue: It's a heart issue. And studying Scriptures like today's passage have helped me better understand how God views my body—which is how I, too, should view it.

As Christians, we often recognize the necessity of tending to our spiritual well-being, but our physical well-being might be an afterthought. On the sixth day of creation, when God created Adam and Eve, He blessed them and told them to be fruitful and multiply, having dominion over all the earth (Genesis 1:26–30). At the end of the day, "God saw everything that He had made, and indeed it was very good" (Genesis 1:31). Our bodies are "fearfully and wonderfully made," in opposition to gnosticism, the idea that our flesh is merely a temporal prison for our eternal souls (Psalm 139:14).

If we want to know with absolute certainty that the Lord values our body, we need to look no further than Jesus, "the Word [who] became flesh and dwelt among us" (John 1:14). In Christ's incarnation, the apostles "beheld His glory, the glory as of the only begotten of the Father, full of grace and truth" (John 1:14).

In 1 Corinthians 6:19–20, Paul teaches that our bodies aren't merely vessels—they're temples of the Holy Spirit. This teaching echoes what Jesus said in John 2:19, after He cleansed the temple. When the Jews asked for a sign to prove that He was the

Christ, He told them, "Destroy this temple, and in three days I will raise it up." The Jews scoffed, but John explains what Jesus meant: "He was speaking of the temple of His body. Therefore, when He had risen from the dead, His disciples remembered that He had said this to them; and they believed the Scripture and the word which Jesus had said" (John 2:21–22).

That Jesus's body was resurrected and ascended into heaven further reinforces the truth that our bodies are made holy in Him, whose blood was shed on the cross to redeem both our souls *and* our bodies. As Job proclaimed, "For I know that my Redeemer lives, and He shall stand at last on the earth; and after my skin is destroyed, this I know, that in my flesh I shall see God, whom I shall see for myself, and my eyes shall behold, and not another" (Job 19:25–27).

When you read through the Bible, you encounter a lot of stories and metaphors about food and drink. This makes sense, because both of these are necessary to sustain life in this age. However, while we're encouraged to care for and nourish the body we've been given, spiritual nourishment is paramount.

At the beginning of His visible ministry, "Jesus was led up by the Spirit into the wilderness to be tempted by the devil. And when He had fasted forty days and forty nights, afterward He was hungry" (Matthew 4:1–2). Satan came to Him and said, "If You are the Son of God, command that these stones become bread" (Matthew 4:3). Jesus, the bread of life Himself, combated the devil's attack by quoting Deuteronomy 8:3: "It is written, 'Man shall not live by bread alone, but by every word that proceeds from the mouth of God'" (John 6:35; Matthew 4:4).

Jesus later preached this same principle in the Sermon on the Mount: "Therefore I say to you, do not worry about your life, what you will eat or what you will drink; nor about your body, what you will put on. Is not life more than food and the body more than clothing?" (Matthew 6:25). His words emphasize that while our physical needs are important, they should never dominate our thinking.

Although our culture sometimes conveys the idea that our dietary choices carry moral weight, the Bible doesn't support this notion. Jesus said, "There is nothing that enters a man from outside which can defile him; but the things which come out of him, those are the things that defile a man.... Whatever enters a man from outside cannot defile him, because it does not enter his heart but his stomach, and is eliminated, thus purifying all foods" (Mark 7:15, 18–19). He reminded His disciples that God is concerned with our hearts first and foremost. Paul wrote in 1 Corinthians 8:8: "But food does not commend us to God; for neither if we eat are we the better, nor if we do not eat are we the worse." Our bodies and food are temporal, yet this doesn't diminish their importance—especially when we make health decisions through the lens of stewardship.

It's impossible for a nation full of unhealthy, sick people to thrive. Our country needs able-bodied people to serve as military personnel, firefighters, and law enforcement officers. We need people who can do hard, manual labor. We need parents and grandparents to have long, healthy lives for their children and grandchildren—and God willing, even great- and great-great-grandchildren—as godly influences.

Paul wrote in Ephesians 2:10, "For we are His workmanship, created in Christ Jesus for good works, which God prepared beforehand that we should walk in them." Let us do everything in our power to optimize our physical health—nourishing, moving, and resting our temples, so we may glorify God in and through them.

Prayer

Heavenly Father, thank You for the gift of our bodies and the Holy Spirit that dwells within them. Please forgive us for the times we've been negligent stewards of our bodies, and help us to make wise choices regarding our spiritual and physical well-being, remembering that when we honor our bodies, we're better able to serve others. As a nation, may we advocate for laws, policies, and systems that support the health and well-being of all Americans. Amen.

For Further Reflection

- What do you think are some detrimental effects that Americans' escalating poor health has had on the country?
- Are there ways you can advocate for better health, whether in your family or community? How would these activities help you love your neighbor?

____

____

____

____

____

____

He comes to judge the nations,
A terror to His foes.
A light of consolations
And blessed hope to those
Who love the Lord's appearing.
O glorious Sun, now come,
Send forth Your beams most cheering,
And guide us safely home.

"O Lord, How Shall I Meet You"

True Riches

Those who trust in their wealth
And boast in the multitude of their riches,
None of them can by any means redeem his brother,
Nor give to God a ransom for him—
For the redemption of their souls is costly,
And it shall cease forever....
Do not be afraid when one becomes rich,
When the glory of his house is increased;
For when he dies he shall carry nothing away;
His glory shall not descend after him.
Though while he lives he blesses himself
(For men will praise you when you do well for yourself),
He shall go to the generation of his fathers;
They shall never see light.

—PSALM 49:6–8, 16–19

The United States is one of the wealthiest nations in the world, so it's not surprising that some of the wealthiest people in the world reside here. In fact, more billionaires live in the United States than in any other country. Each year, different publications release their lists ranking the wealthiest Americans, stating the individuals' net worth, at times even describing how they accumulated that wealth and how they're spending it.

We see evidence of this wealth every time we turn on the TV or go online. Traditional media is seemingly obsessed with detailing the exploits of the "haves," and social media gives people their own outlets to display their wealth—glamourous vacations, extravagant yachts, designer clothes, attendance at high-profile events, and so on.

In our materialistic world, the allure of wealth can mesmerize us. The affluent lifestyles, exquisite possessions, and status symbols that surround us can lead us to feel inadequate, disregarding the many blessings God has bestowed upon us. Or we might begin to envy those who have more than we do, in violation of the commandment: "You shall not covet your neighbor's house; you shall not covet your neighbor's wife, nor his male servant, nor his female servant, nor his ox, nor his donkey, nor anything that is your neighbor's" (Exodus 20:17).

Since wealth can be such a snare, the Bible contains many passages that address money and our relationship to it. Psalm 49 provides us with a clear perspective not only of the futility of wealth but also of the assurance we have in God.

In verse 16, the psalmist wrote that we shouldn't be afraid when we see other people gaining riches, "when the glory of his house is increased." Oftentimes, with wealth comes the illusion of power. It can feel like those who have money also wield disproportionate control over our world, influencing everything from politics and justice to the economy and culture. As it says in verse 18, "Men will praise you when you do well for yourself," because human beings desire alignment with the wealthy and powerful.

Yet God is ultimately the One who's in control of all these things. No matter how vast the possessions of the rich, Psalm 49:17 and 19 remind us that "when he dies he shall carry nothing away; his glory shall not descend after him.... He shall go to the generation of his fathers; they shall never see light." Wealth is transient, and it won't accompany us beyond the grave. This truth is reinforced in 1 Timothy 6:6–8: "Now godliness with contentment is great gain. For we brought nothing into this world, and it is certain we can carry nothing out. And having food and clothing, with these we shall be content." Paul reminds us that having our basic needs of food and clothing is enough, and that pursuing God is the greatest need of all.

In another psalm we read, "A little that a righteous man has is better than the riches of many wicked. For the arms of the wicked shall be broken, but the Lord upholds the righteous" (Psalm 37:16–17). While wealth impresses the world, it's no indication of the Lord's favor.

Either a lack or abundance of money can lead us astray. Proverbs 30:8–9 says, "Give me neither poverty nor riches—feed me with the food allotted to me; lest I be full and deny You, and say, 'Who is the Lord?' Or lest I be poor and steal, and profane the name of my God." When we feel that we don't have adequate funds for our basic needs, we're tempted to take what doesn't belong to us, instead of trusting the Lord to provide our daily bread. In contrast, when we have all the money we need and then some, we're tempted to trust in ourselves instead of God, believing that we've accumulated our possessions by our own power. Jesus warned of this danger in Matthew 6:24: "No one can serve two masters; for either he will hate the one and love the other, or else he will be loyal to the one and despise the other. You cannot serve God and mammon."

Earlier in the Gospel of Matthew, Jesus told His listeners, "Do not lay up for yourselves treasures on earth, where moth and rust destroy and where thieves break in and steal; but lay up for yourselves treasures in heaven, where neither moth nor rust destroys and where thieves do not break in and steal. For where your treasure is, there your heart will be also" (Matthew 6:19–21). When we view our lives through the lens of eternity, we realize that, as Job confessed, everything we have here is fleeting (Job 1:21). Not only this, but it pales in comparison to the riches we have now in the Lord's kingdom and the treasures that await us in heaven.

Wealth may provide a sense of security, yet it can neither prevent our death nor save our souls, as the psalmist declared in today's reading: "None of them can by any means redeem his brother, nor give to God a ransom for him—for the redemption of their souls is costly" (Psalm 49:7–8). True redemption only comes through Jesus Christ. He was the One "who gave Himself a ransom for all," paying the highest price for our salvation by His death on the cross (1 Timothy 2:6).

Let us not find security in personal wealth or the wealth of nations, but in the blood of Jesus Christ. In Him, we have true riches that transcend anything and everything we have here on earth.

Prayer

Lord, we confess that at times we've trusted in ourselves and in worldly things instead of relying solely on You to provide all we need to sustain us, in this life and the next. Please forgive us for this sin and allow us to find our contentment and worth in You, not in earthly riches. And may we give thanks and praise to our Lord and Savior Jesus Christ, who paid the price for our salvation. In His name we pray. Amen.

For Further Reflection

- How can you appreciate and celebrate the blessings others receive, financial or otherwise, without feeling envious of them?
- Are there any ways that your life reflects a trust in wealth rather than in God? What steps can you take today to strengthen your focus on eternal treasures?

Love Not the World

Do not love the world or the things in the world.
If anyone loves the world, the love of the Father is not in him.
For all that is in the world—the lust of the flesh, the lust of the eyes, and the pride of life—is not of the Father but is of the world.
And the world is passing away, and the lust of it;
but he who does the will of God abides forever.

—1 JOHN 2:15–17

William Wordsworth, one of the most famous British Romantic poets, wrote a piece titled "The World Is Too Much with Us." In this fourteen-line sonnet, he expressed a longing for humanity to be less concerned with acquiring goods and money and for a return to simpler times, when people were enamored with the natural world and all its wonders.

While the Apostle John wouldn't necessarily have shared Wordsworth's belief that the natural world was somehow superior to the man-made world, John likely would have agreed that "the world is too much with us."

If what Solomon wrote in Ecclesiastes 1:9 is true, and "there is nothing new under the sun," then we know that what was true during his time was also true during John's time and remains true in our time. Solomon was a man who knew a lot about "the lust of the flesh, the lust of the eyes, and the pride of life" (1 John 2:16), yet he declared all these things "vanity and grasping for the wind" (Ecclesiastes 1:14).

During John's lifetime, the Roman Empire was known for its decadence and pagan worship, and all of this is the same in our world: lust, pride, decadence, pagan worship, and so forth.

The things we want to feel and the pleasures we want to experience, the things we want to see and the words we want to hear, can be sinful allures that our flesh finds irresistible. We have endless opportunities for instant gratification for any and every desire, and the ease with which we can access these opportunities makes resisting temptation all the more challenging.

Even the things God intended for good can become snares. For instance, we yearn to have a sense of identity and belonging. We're created in the image of God and meant to be in community with one another. Yet the world entices us to renounce God's image and adopt identities and communities that coerce us to compromise our Christian faith and values.

The evil foe whispers, "Has God indeed said...?" making us doubt and question God's truth (Genesis 3:1–6). We might say or think things like the following: If we're supposed to "hate the sin but love the sinner," it's okay to be an "ally," right? The government says it's legal to smoke pot or partake of other legal substances, so there's no harm in it. I just follow that person's social media account because I like their photographs—I don't support their lifestyle choices.

Also, the busyness of modern life can easily distract us, drawing us away from spending time with God in worship, in

His Word, and in prayer. This distance can leave us vulnerable to the world and its abundant charms, less able to discern God's will and attain clarity about what our priorities should be.

But as John makes clear, love for the world and love for the Father cannot coexist.

If you read through 1 John, you'll find the word "love" dozens of times. And if you've ever read the Gospel of John, that would come as no surprise. Love is a focal point of John's writings, including what is probably the most famous Bible verse, John 3:16: "For God so loved that world that He gave His only begotten Son, that whoever believes in Him should not perish but have everlasting life."

Notice, however, that the word "world" is also included in this verse. The word in the biblical Greek is "cosmos," and the same word is used later, when John shares Jesus's final prayer before His arrest in the Garden of Gethsemane. In the last petition, Jesus prays for all believers: "I do not pray for these alone, but also for those who will believe in Me through their word; that they all may be one, as You, Father, are in Me, and I in You; that they also may be one in Us, that the world may believe that You sent Me.... O righteous Father! The world has not known You, but I have known You; and these have known that You sent Me" (John 17:20–21, 25).

In 1 John 2:15–17, the disciple whom Jesus loved merely shared what he had learned from the mouth of Jesus: The world doesn't know Him, but those who believe in Him know Him and abide with Him.

When we seek God first—attending worship to hear His Word and receive His sacraments, uplifting other believers, being intentional about what and who influences us, and sharing Christ's love with the world—we are aligned with His will and purposes for our lives. Titus 2:11–13 provides an encouraging exhortation for those who call on the name of the Lord: "For the grace of God that brings salvation has appeared to all men, teaching us that, denying ungodliness and worldly lusts, we should live soberly, righteously, and godly in the present age, looking for the blessed hope and glorious appearing of our great God and Savior Jesus Christ."

Solomon's kingdom only lasted as long as his reign (forty years), and most of Israel was stripped from the son who ascended the throne after his death. Then, about three and a half centuries later, that kingdom was wiped out by the Babylonians under King Nebuchadnezzar.

The Roman Empire existed for a little over four hundred years.

The United States celebrates its 250th birthday in 2026.

As 1 John 2:17 tells us, "the world is passing away." Although we love our country and are committed to praying for it, we need to remember that it won't last forever.

What will last forever is God's heavenly kingdom. Let us abide *in* Him, so we may abide *with* Him, for all eternity.

Prayer

Father, we confess that we are often drawn to love the things of this world, sometimes more than we are drawn to love You. May we repent of placing anything above You, and of aligning ourselves with anything that is not of You. Let us not cling to the things of this world, which is passing away, but to our Lord and Savior Jesus Christ, whose kingdom is eternal. To Him be all glory, forever and ever. Amen.

For Further Reflection

- What "things of the world" do you tend to love? Why do those things appeal to you? How do those things draw you away from God? What can you do to minimize their negative effect on your life?
- How can we support and commend our nation's leaders when they take action that supports Christian values and beliefs?

Fighting Our True Enemy

Finally, my brethren, be strong in the Lord and in the power of His might. Put on the whole armor of God, that you may be able to stand against the wiles of the devil. For we do not wrestle against flesh and blood, but against principalities, against powers, against the rulers of the darkness of this age, against spiritual hosts of wickedness in the heavenly places. Therefore take up the whole armor of God, that you may be able to withstand in the evil day, and having done all, to stand.

—EPHESIANS 6:10–13

In our nation's current climate, it can be easy for us to feel like our biggest battles are against cultural deviancy and political misconduct. But make no mistake: While those who further such things are an outward manifestation of our enemy, they're not our true enemy. The true enemy is the devil, our adversary who "walks about like a roaring lion, seeking whom he may devour" (1 Peter 5:8).

The opening chapter of the book of Job contains a fascinating scene of conversation between God and Satan, which helps us better understand how he operates. When the angels "present[ed] themselves before the Lord," Satan arrived with them (Job 1:6). God asked him, "From where do you come?" to which

Satan replied, "From going to and fro on the earth, and from walking back and forth on it" (Job 1:7). In His omniscience, God knew where the devil had been, but He provided an opportunity for prideful Satan to share his whereabouts.

After this conversation, the Lord allowed Satan to torment Job, of whom He said, "There is none like him on the earth, a blameless and upright man, one who fears God and shuns evil" (Job 1:8). During Satan's first attack, he destroyed all of Job's worldly possessions plus his ten children. In the second attack, he destroyed Job's health. Even though God permitted these things to happen, He set a limit on the power to harm: "Behold, he is in your hand, but spare his life" (Job 2:6).

It can be hard to understand why God allowed these tragedies to befall Job. Even Jesus was subject to Satan's torment, when He was tempted after fasting forty days and forty nights in the wilderness. However, while we sometimes fail to resist Satan's attacks, Jesus perfectly resisted them (Matthew 4:1–11; Luke 4:1–13).

Ephesians 6:12 reminds us that we're not fighting against "flesh and blood," but "against principalities, against powers, against the rulers of the darkness of this age, against spiritual hosts of wickedness." We're engaged in a spiritual battle against the evil spirits that oppose God and His truth.

Keeping this reality in mind can help us maintain a proper perspective when we find ourselves in conflict with individuals, the culture, or civil leaders. Satan can use each to further his agenda, which is to destroy human beings, both physically and spiritually. As Jesus said of him, "He was a murderer from the beginning, and does not stand in the truth, because there is no truth in him. When he speaks a lie, he speaks from his own resources, for he is a liar and the father of it" (John 8:44).

Throughout history, leaders who reject the Lord and His will have been used, knowingly or unknowingly, to further Satan's perverse ends. Reading through the Old Testament, you find dozens of examples of evil leaders, which included many of Israel's own kings. One of the most wicked of all was Manasseh of Judah.

When he ascended the throne, "he also built altars in the house of the Lord, of which the Lord had said, 'In Jerusalem I will put My name.' And he built altars for all the host of heaven in the two courts of the house of the Lord. Also he made his son pass through the fire, practiced soothsaying, used witchcraft, and consulted spiritists and mediums. He did much evil in the sight of the Lord, to provoke Him to anger" (2 Kings 21:4–6). Based on these evil deeds, it was said that he "seduced [the people] to do more evil than the nations whom the Lord had destroyed before the children of Israel" (2 Kings 21:9).

In the New Testament, one of the clearest examples of a leader being used to undermine God's will was when King Herod ordered the slaughter of the innocents. After the wise men told Herod that they had come to worship "He who has been born King of the Jews," he instructed them to return to him (Matthew 2:2, 8). But in a dream, they were warned not to go back to Herod. When the king learned of this, he "was exceedingly angry; and he sent forth and put to death all the male children who were in Bethlehem and in all its districts, from two years old and under, according to the time which he had determined from the wise men" (Matthew 2:16).

Thankfully, Joseph also had received a dream that warned him to flee with Mary and Jesus to Egypt, only returning after Herod died (Matthew 2:19–20). Thus, Satan's plan to destroy the Christ was thwarted.

Both Manasseh and Herod prove that compromised leadership corrupts the gifts of government and nation that the Lord established for the good of mankind.

As we battle against the forces of darkness, we don our armor that Paul listed in Ephesians 6:14–17. One of the items provided is "the sword of the Spirit, which is the word of God" (Ephesians 6:17). God's truth—especially the truth that Jesus Christ, God incarnate, was born, died, and resurrected—is the truth that defends us against all danger.

Although Paul doesn't specifically include prayer as part of the armor, he still considered it an essential part of our defense, instructing us to "[pray] always with all prayer and supplication in the Spirit, being watchful to this end with all perseverance and supplication for all the saints" (Ephesians 6:18).

Satan may attack us, but Jesus Christ has already won the victory in His crucifixion, for "now is the judgment of this world; now the ruler of this world will be cast out" (John 12:31). Let us rest secure in this truth, stand strong with God's weapons, live in confidence, and trust that God has equipped us to withstand the evils of this age.

Prayer

Mighty Lord, help us to see that the cultural and political decline in our nation is part of a spiritual battle between the powers of darkness and light. Please equip us with Your full armor every day, so we may withstand the enemy's attacks. When we struggle, remind us that victory is ours in Christ Jesus, who on the cross defeated sin, death, and the devil. In His holy name we pray. Amen.

For Further Reflection

- Do you think it is easier for Satan to manipulate people in positions of power? Why or why not?
- Why do you think we sometimes get caught up in earthly drama and lose sight of the spiritual battle?

Being Generous with Our Possessions

Honor the Lord with your possessions,
And with the firstfruits of all your increase;
So your barns will be filled with plenty,
And your vats will overflow with new wine.

—PROVERBS 3:9–10

Americans can be charitable, generous people, sharing our time, talents, and treasures with churches, nonprofits, and other entities. On the flip side, Americans can be extremely covetous and greedy, embracing a consumerist culture founded on materialism. This is evidenced in many things, from the numerous storage units springing up all around and white-collar crimes like embezzlement to phishing scams that steal people's money and shoplifting. Each of these breaks God's commandments not to covet or steal.

Proverbs 3:9 calls us to "honor the Lord with [our] possessions, and with the firstfruits of all [our] increase." This verse tells us the importance of acknowledging that God is the source of all blessings, including possessions. Our culture's obsession with wealth leads to cycles of mass consumption that can distort that truth and warp our understanding of what it means to be a good steward.

The first time an offering is made in the Bible is in Genesis 4:3–5: "And in the process of time it came to pass that Cain brought an offering of the fruit of the ground to the Lord. Abel also brought of the firstborn of his flock and of their fat. And the Lord respected Abel and his offering, but He did not respect Cain and his offering. And Cain was very angry, and his countenance fell." On the surface, it's easy to say, "Well, of course the Lord preferred Abel's offering—a sacrifice of livestock is much greater than some fruit!" But that overlooks the crux of the matter.

Hebrews 11:4 says, "By faith Abel offered to God a more excellent sacrifice than Cain, through which he obtained witness that he was righteous, God testifying of his gifts; and through it he being dead still speaks." It wasn't that Abel obtained righteousness because he offered an "excellent sacrifice" but that he "obtained witness that he was righteous" because he brought an offering in faith. Based on this, we surmise that Cain's offering was made in absence of faith, which is why the Lord didn't respect it.

In Luke, Jesus told a parable about a rich man. He prefaced the story with these words: "Take heed and beware of covetousness, for one's life does not consist in the abundance of the things he possesses" (Luke 12:15). The rich man in the parable was a farmer whose ground yielded a bumper crop. He needed to figure out how to store the food, so he decided to tear down his barns and build new, bigger ones to store the harvest he intended to live on for years. "But God said to [the man], 'Fool! This night your soul will be required of you; then whose will those things be which you have provided?'" (Luke 12:20). Jesus concluded by saying, "So is he who lays up treasure for himself, and is not rich toward God" (Luke 12:21).

This parable is a cautionary tale against greed and a selfish pursuit of wealth. Instead of recognizing the Lord as the provider of this blessing and sharing his abundance, the rich man planned to hoard it. After his life was demanded of him, he wouldn't be able to enjoy the possessions anyway.

His folly reflects the words found in Deuteronomy 8, in which God warned the Israelites of pride after they had entered the Promised Land: "When you have eaten and are full, and have built beautiful houses and dwell in them; and when your herds and your flocks multiply, and your silver and your gold are multiplied, and all that you have is multiplied... [Beware lest] then you say in your heart, 'My power and the might of my hand have gained me this wealth.' And you shall remember the Lord your God, for it is He who gives you power to get wealth" (Deuteronomy 8:12–13, 17–18).

In contrast to the rich man, we have Job. After he lost everything he had—his livestock, his servants, and his children—he "arose, tore his robe, and shaved his head; and he fell to the ground and worshiped. And he said: 'Naked I came from my mother's womb, and naked shall I return there. The Lord gave, and the Lord has taken away; blessed be the name of the Lord.' In all this Job did not sin nor charge God with wrong" (Job

1:20–22). When tragedy struck, Job didn't ask, "Why me?" or blame God. Instead, he spoke a confession of faith with a profound understanding of the nature of possessions.

America's culture encourages individuals to be less like Job and more like the rich man, tempting us to find our identity in material goods instead of in Christ. This consumer mentality fosters anxiety and discontent, creating a void we try to fill in vain, because it can only be filled by God.

To combat this temptation, we look to the Bible for wisdom. In his letter to the Philippians, Paul wrote: "Not that I speak in regard to need, for I have learned in whatever state I am, to be content: I know how to be abased, and I know how to abound. Everywhere and in all things I have learned both to be full and to be hungry, both to abound and to suffer need. I can do all things through Christ who strengthens me" (Philippians 4:11–13). Paul teaches us the truth that security and contentment come not from possessions and wealth but from fellowship with God.

Our Lord and Savior Jesus Christ says, "And do not seek what you should eat or what you should drink, nor have an anxious mind. For all these things the nations of the world seek after, and your Father knows that you need these things. But seek the kingdom of God, and all these things shall be added to you" (Luke 12:29–31).

May we always seek God first, knowing and trusting that when we do, He provides everything we need—in this life and the next.

Prayer

Generous Lord, true wealth is found in fellowship with You. Help us to honor You with our possessions, and enable us to resist the temptations of materialism and greed. As You cultivate hearts of gratitude within us, may we live with contentment and share the riches of the hope and joy we have in Jesus Christ. Amen.

For Further Reflection

- In what ways does a consumerist culture affect our country?
- How would our nation look if people were more focused on seeking God and serving others than on acquiring material things?

Kings shall fall down before Him
And gold and incense bring;
All nations shall adore Him,
His praise all people sing.
To Him shall prayer unceasing
And daily vows ascend;
His kingdom still increasing,
A kingdom without end.

“Hail to the Lord’s Anointed”

Put Away Evil and Do Good

Wash yourselves, make yourselves clean;
Put away the evil of your doings from before My eyes.
Cease to do evil,
Learn to do good;
Seek justice,
Rebuke the oppressor;
Defend the fatherless,
Plead for the widow.

—ISAIAH 1:16–17

Artistic renditions of justice are often personified as a woman. In one hand, she holds a scale, which represents balance in applying the law. In her other hand, she holds a sword, representing the state's power, as well as protection and authority. Typically, a blindfold covers her eyes, conveying the idea that justice should be impartial.

Statues of justice can be found in front of many courthouses throughout the country, and the US Supreme Court building is no exception. Within the walls of the highest court in the land, decisions are handed down that have far-reaching effects. Some of the court's rulings have been wise and just; others have been foolish and detrimental.

America's judicial system has both strengths and weaknesses. At its best, it holds criminals accountable, protects people's rights, ensures fair trials, and upholds the law. At its worst, it applies the law unequally, which leads to injustice. These failures demonstrate that even the best judicial system falls short of the Lord's perfect justice.

The word "justice" is mentioned in the New King James Version of the Bible 136 times, indicating its importance to God. The first time it's used is in Genesis 18:19, before the destruction of Sodom and Gomorrah. God said of Abraham, "For I have known him, in order that he may command his children and his household after him, that they keep the way of the Lord, to do righteousness and justice, that the Lord may bring to Abraham what He has spoken to him." Justice would be a hallmark of the faithful, beginning with the choosing of Abraham.

That was reinforced in the Mosaic law. Throughout Deuteronomy, we find several mentions of justice, including the following: "For the Lord your God is God of gods and Lord of lords, the great God, mighty and awesome, who shows no partiality nor takes a bribe. He administers justice for the fatherless and the widow, and loves the stranger, giving him food and clothing" (Deuteronomy 10:17–18). God is not only the perfect lawgiver but also the perfect judge. His law and justice are the standards against which all things must be measured.

These verses from Deuteronomy show us that God is the only one capable of perfect impartiality when administering justice. A few chapters later, He addressed the need for His people to be unmoved by those with power, money, or influence:

"You shall appoint judges and officers in all your gates, which the Lord your God gives you, according to your tribes, and they shall judge the people with just judgment. You shall not pervert justice; you shall not show partiality, nor take a bribe, for a bribe blinds the eyes of the wise and twists the words of the righteous" (Deuteronomy 16:18–19; see also Leviticus 19:15).

After the Exodus, there was need for someone to serve in this role during the forty years of wilderness wandering: "Moses sat to judge the people; and the people stood before Moses from morning until evening" (Exodus 18:13). But when his father-in-law, Jethro, arrived, he asked, "What is this thing that you are doing for the people? Why do you alone sit, and all the people stand before you from morning until evening?" And Moses said, "Because the people come to me to inquire of God. When they have a difficulty, they come to me, and I judge between one and another; and I make known the statutes of God and His laws" (Exodus 18:14–16).

Jethro realized this system was unsustainable, so he advised Moses to instruct the people in God's laws, but to "select from all the people able men, such as fear God, men of truth, hating covetousness; and place such over them to be rulers of thousands, rulers of hundreds, rulers of fifties, and rulers of tens. And let them judge the people at all times. Then it will be that every great matter they shall bring to you, but every small matter they themselves shall judge" (Exodus 18:21–22).

Moses heeded Jethro's wise advice. His follow-through is a reminder that we need to delegate. However, Moses wasn't to hand over this responsibility to just anyone. The appointees had to meet specific criteria, which included fearing God, loving truth, and hating covetousness. These are the same kinds of people we want to lead our legal system, as justice uncoupled from God's law leads to injustice.

Not long after the Israelites entered the Promised Land, they were blessed with judges—Gideon, Deborah, Samson, and others. The description of Deborah functioning as judge provides insight into how they served: "Now Deborah, a prophetess, the wife of Lapidoth, was judging Israel at that time. And she would sit under the palm tree of Deborah between Ramah and Bethel in the mountains of Ephraim. And the children of Israel came up to her for judgment" (Judges 4:4–5). Like Moses, the judges applied God's law to arbitrate between the Israelites' disputes.

Following the period of the judges was the monarchy, Saul being anointed as Israel's first king. After him came David, followed by Solomon. Solomon was renowned for his wise judgments, but during his son's reign, the kingdom split in two. From that point onward, the people lived under a mixture of good and bad kings.

Time and time again, the Lord sent prophets to call His people to repentance and return to Him and His law. One of the most common charges leveled against the people was their lack of justice. For instance, Amos spoke this word: "Therefore, because you tread down the poor and take grain taxes from him, though you have built houses of hewn stone, yet you shall not dwell in them; you have planted pleasant vineyards, but you shall not drink wine from them. For I know your manifold transgressions and your mighty sins: afflicting the just and taking bribes; diverting the poor from justice at the gate" (Amos 5:11–12). The Israelites were doing what God had specifically commanded them *not* to do, and they would face His wrath.

When we reflect on the Israelites' challenges in keeping God's law, we might recognize our own failures to pursue justice, whether in our communities, state, or nation. Christians have a responsibility to advocate for those who are unable to advocate for themselves, including through the legal system. We can pursue careers in law and become attorneys and judges. We can support legal aid organizations—particularly those that defend religious freedoms. And, of course, we can pray for those in positions of judicial authority throughout the country, and bring our petitions before the divine Judge, for "He is the Rock, His work is perfect; for all His ways are justice, a God of truth and without injustice; righteous and upright is He" (Deuteronomy 32:4).

Prayer

Dear Lord, "righteousness and justice are the foundation of Your throne; mercy and truth go before Your face" (Psalm 89:14). We confess that we often fail to properly administer justice throughout our land. May You raise up lawyers, prosecutors, defenders, and other legal professionals who love You and Your Word, that they may protect the innocent and punish the guilty. We ask this in Jesus's precious and holy name. Amen.

For Further Reflection

- Can you think of any recent legal injustices you have heard about? What was unjust about the situation? How do you think the situation would have been handled if God's law had been applied?
- In what ways does our legal system support Christian values and beliefs? In what ways does it undermine or outright oppose them?

Loving Our Enemies in a Divided World

You have heard that it was said, "You shall love your neighbor and hate your enemy." But I say to you, love your enemies, bless those who curse you, do good to those who hate you, and pray for those who spitefully use you and persecute you, that you may be sons of your Father in heaven; for He makes His sun rise on the evil and on the good, and sends rain on the just and on the unjust.

—MATTHEW 5:43–45

"Oh, I could never be friends with anyone who voted for that person."

"My uncle got uninvited to Thanksgiving dinner because of his political beliefs."

"I read that someone lost their job because they posted something on social media that their employer didn't like."

Division seems to dominate every American setting. The tension permeates conversations, social media interactions, workplaces, and even families. In this environment, the idea of loving our enemies can seem challenging, if not impossible.

How can I love someone who has declared me an enemy because I don't think the same way she does? How can I bless someone who curses me because I say abortion is evil? How can I do good to someone who hates me because I didn't vote for her preferred candidate? How can I pray for someone who persecutes me because she hates God and thinks anyone who believes in Him is either stupid or delusional?

In the Sermon on the Mount, Jesus calls us to do precisely this: "Love your enemies, bless those who curse you, do good to those who hate you, and pray for those who spitefully use you and persecute you" (Matthew 5:44). As individual Christians, when we clash with others, instead of treating them with disdain, we're challenged to demonstrate the Father's grace and mercy. When we do so, we allow His light to shine forth into the world's darkness.

At the same time, we have a responsibility to our neighbor in need not to act with initial aggression, yet with responsive force. For instance, my husband might turn his cheek if he's being harmed, but he's called to defend me and our children against those who seek to harm us. In either case, he's truly loving his neighbor as God has commanded.

Romans 12:18 says, "If it is possible, as much as depends on you, live peaceably with all men." All human beings are sinful, so conflict is inevitable, including with those we love. When someone offends us, it can be tempting to respond in kind. That temptation is especially powerful with electronic communication, which allows us to detach ourselves from the impact our words have on others.

We should avoid initiating conflict or provoking people to anger and instead strive to be peacemakers: "Blessed are the peacemakers, for they shall be called sons of God" (Matthew 5:9). Again, our pursuit of peace with others reflects our fellowship with the Heavenly Father, and the eternal Peacemaker, Jesus Christ.

Because of Jesus's death on the cross, we have peace with God in the forgiveness of our sins. Therefore, we're enabled to do as we pray in the Lord's Prayer: "And forgive us our sins, for we also forgive everyone who is indebted to us" (Luke 11:4). If we acknowledge the depth of our sin, we're able to love others more, for "to whom little is forgiven, the same loves little" (Luke 7:47). Self-righteousness prohibits our ability to love others in the way Jesus teaches us.

Lest we think we're better than others, we're reminded that God "makes His sun rise on the evil and on the good, and sends rain on the just and on the unjust" (Matthew 5:45). If not for our faith in Jesus, we'd be in the same position as those who mistreat us, as Paul reminds us: "For we ourselves were also once foolish, disobedient, deceived, serving various lusts and pleasures, living in malice and envy, hateful and hating one another. But when the kindness and the love of God our Savior toward man appeared, not by works of righteousness which we have done, but according to His mercy He saved us, through the washing of regeneration and renewing of the Holy Spirit, whom He poured out on us abundantly through Jesus Christ our Savior" (Titus 3:3–6).

In the Gospel of John, Jesus warned His disciples that they would face opposition and hatred from the world: "If the world hates you, you know that it hated Me before it hated you. If you were of the world, the world would love its own. Yet because you are not of the world, but I chose you out of the world, therefore the world hates you" (John 15:18–19). Rather than retaliate or respond with anger, we should follow the example He Himself provided, as well as His first martyr, Stephen.

Before Jesus was crucified, He endured a gauntlet of unimaginable pain and torment. He was betrayed by Judas Iscariot, abandoned by His disciples, denied by Peter, falsely accused, spat on, slapped, punched, lashed with a whip, and pierced by a crown of thorns. Any one of those things would be excruciating to endure—mentally, emotionally, and physically. Yet after He was hoisted on the cross, He prayed, "Father, forgive them, for they know not what they do" (Luke 23:34).

Similarly, when Stephen, one of Jesus's disciples, was being stoned to death by the Jews, he prayed as Jesus did: "Lord, do not charge them with this sin" (Acts 7:60). Stephen devoutly embodied one of Jesus's teachings from the Sermon on the Mount: "But I tell you not to resist an evil person. But whoever slaps you on your right cheek, turn the other to him also" (Matthew 5:39).

Although we may never be called to forfeit our lives for the Gospel, we should be prepared to do so, knowing that this is Christ's will for us: "Then Jesus said to His disciples, 'If anyone desires to come after Me, let him deny himself, and take up his cross, and follow Me. For whoever desires to save his life will lose it, but whoever loses his life for My sake will find it'" (Matthew 16:24–25).

While disagreements and conflict are inevitable in our families, communities, and nation, we can apply Jesus's example to every situation, keeping in mind that "a soft answer turns away wrath, but a harsh word stirs up anger" (Proverbs 15:1).

Prayer

Heavenly Father, help us embody Christ's love, transforming our hearts so we're eager to pray for our enemies—remembering that we, too, were once Your enemies. Please allow us to be peacemakers in our communities and our nation, to heal divisions and be the salt of the earth You've called us to be. In the name of Jesus, who lives and reigns with You and the Holy Spirit, one God now and forever. Amen.

For Further Reflection

- How do you typically respond when you disagree or have a conflict with someone? How might you respond differently based on today's Bible passages?
- In what ways can Christians serve as peacemakers in our divided nation?

____

____

____

____

____

____

____

Watchmen for the Lord

So you, son of man: I have made you a watchman for the house of Israel; therefore you shall hear a word from My mouth and warn them for Me. When I say to the wicked, "O wicked man, you shall surely die!" and you do not speak to warn the wicked from his way, that wicked man shall die in his iniquity; but his blood I will require at your hand. Nevertheless if you warn the wicked to turn from his way, and he does not turn from his way, he shall die in his iniquity; but you have delivered your soul.

—EZEKIEL 33:7–9

His eyes scanned the horizon, squinting against the glare of the setting sun. A light breeze offered some relief from the day's waning heat as he deeply inhaled the early evening air. High up on the city wall, his position allowed him to see for miles in every direction.

He knew how critical his role was to the city's safety. All throughout his watch, he'd keep his eyes trained on the horizon, vigilantly seeking signs of any potential dangers.

And he knew that his awesome responsibility was an honor, because fulfilling his duty protected the entire community. Their lives were in his hands. If he failed to spot trouble or sound the alarm, everyone in the city was at risk.

Based on the potential dire outcomes, one can see that only someone with a heightened sense of duty to his fellow human beings should be permitted to serve as a watchman.

Because of the role watchmen played in ancient Israel, God used this metaphor in regard to his prophet Ezekiel. While watchmen were crucial to keeping the Israelites physically safe, Ezekiel's service as a spiritual watchman was even more crucial, because it had eternal consequences.

The Lord, in His mercy, appointed Ezekiel and gave him a serious mandate: "You shall hear a word from My mouth and warn them for Me" (Ezekiel 33:7). As Israel's watchman, he was tasked with the sacred duty of sounding the alarm, warning his countrymen of danger and destruction on the horizon.

If Ezekiel warns "the wicked to turn from his way" to avert God's impending judgment, and "he does not turn from his way," then the wicked alone is responsible for the outcome: "He shall die in his iniquity" (Ezekiel 33:9). The prophet won't be held accountable for such as these. However, if Ezekiel neglects his duty, and does not "speak to warn the wicked from his way, that wicked man shall die in his iniquity," but the Lord would also hold Ezekiel responsible (Ezekiel 33:8).

To be a prophet and watchman of the Lord is a daunting task.

The Watchman par excellence is the Lord Himself. We get a picture of this in the parable of the prodigal. In Luke 15:11–32, Jesus told the story of a son who wanted his share of the inheritance. In essence, he wished his father dead because, of course, you can only receive an inheritance after someone dies.

The son then journeyed to a distant land, squandered his inheritance, and ended up so impoverished that he could only find work feeding slop to pigs—and even the pigs had more to eat than he did.

Finally, he realized that he should go home, confess his wrongdoing, and throw himself on his father's mercy. He determined that it would be preferable to be a hired hand in his father's house than to continue on his current path. Thus, he set off toward home. "But when he was still a great way off, his father saw him and had compassion, and ran and fell on his neck and kissed him" (Luke 15:20).

The Bible doesn't indicate how the father knew the son was coming from such a distance. Had he posted someone, or even multiple people, to keep an eye out for his wayward son? Or was he himself standing watch, staring at the horizon and yearning for the familiar silhouette of his son to appear? Either way, the father made sure that whenever his son returned, he was ready to run to him and welcome him back into his household.

Like the father in the parable, God yearns for His children to turn from evil to Him. As He said in Ezekiel 33:11, "As I live...I have no pleasure in the death of the wicked, but that the wicked turn from his way and live. Turn, turn from your evil ways! For why should you die, O house of Israel?"

We're similar to Ezekiel in our responsibility to our fellow citizens, as watchmen in our communities. Our world is rife with moral ambiguity, societal decay, and godlessness. Like the wicked in Ezekiel's day, many people in our society don't realize they're lost, blind to the imminent dangers surrounding them. We do no one, including ourselves, any favors when we don't call out sin or neglect to assert God's truth while the world "call[s] evil good, and good evil" (Isaiah 5:20). Just like Ezekiel, we're not to sit on the sidelines—we're to be bearers of light and defenders of righteousness, compelled to warn others of the Lord's coming wrath.

We can speak out against sin with grace and love and share the wondrous truth that Jesus Christ died on the cross for all sins. We can tell of the Lord's boundless mercy and forgiveness, so it may be said of every lost soul who repents, "None of his sins which he has committed shall be remembered against him; he has done what is lawful and right; he shall surely live" (Ezekiel 33:16).

Prayer

Heavenly Father, thank You for the awesome responsibility You have given us as watchmen in this world. Help us remain alert and aware of the world around us. Give us the courage and fortitude to speak Your truth in love, pointing others toward the salvation offered through Jesus Christ. In His name we pray. Amen.

For Further Reflection

- Have you ever warned someone that they needed to turn away from a sin? If so, how did that person respond? Have you ever been on the receiving end of such a warning? If so, how did you respond?
- In what ways can you boldly speak the truth in love to people in your community, pointing them toward Christ and the salvation found only in Him?

Unity in God's Eternal Kingdom

After these things I looked, and behold, a great multitude which no one could number, of all nations, tribes, peoples, and tongues, standing before the throne and before the Lamb, clothed with white robes, with palm branches in their hands, and crying out with a loud voice, saying, "Salvation belongs to our God who sits on the throne, and to the Lamb!" All the angels stood around the throne and the elders and the four living creatures, and fell on their faces before the throne and worshiped God, saying:
"Amen! Blessing and glory and wisdom,
Thanksgiving and honor and power and might,
Be to our God forever and ever.
Amen."

—REVELATION 7:9–12

We began at the beginning, so we shall end at the end. But it's not really the end.

It's the beginning of the time that all of creation eagerly anticipates: when Jesus Christ, the Lamb of God, will return in glory and "make all things new" (Revelation 21:5).

This future eternal kingdom reaches back to His incarnation: "For unto us a Child is born, unto us a Son is given; and the government will be upon His shoulder. And His name will be called Wonderful, Counselor, Mighty God, Everlasting Father,

Prince of Peace. Of the increase of His government and peace there will be no end, upon the throne of David and over His kingdom, to order it and establish it with judgment and justice from that time forward, even forever. The zeal of the Lord of hosts will perform this" (Isaiah 9:6–7). Only Jesus fulfills the criteria listed in these verses, because only He can bring peace—between men and between God and men.

As we meditate on these verses from Revelation, we can ponder the awesome image of "a great multitude which no one could number, of all nations, tribes, peoples, and tongues" (Revelation 7:9). These saints are clothed in white robes, waving palm branches and shouting, "Salvation belongs to our God who sits on the throne, and to the Lamb!" (Revelation 7:10). The scene brings to mind Christ's triumphal entry into Jerusalem on Palm Sunday, when Zechariah's prophecy was fulfilled: "Rejoice greatly, O daughter of Zion! Shout, O daughter of Jerusalem! Behold, your King is coming to you; he is just and having salvation, lowly and riding on a donkey, a colt, the foal of a donkey" (Zechariah 9:9). Jesus Christ, the King of all creation, entered the holy city not as a conquering tyrant but as a humble servant bringing peace. And by the end of that week, He'd pay the ultimate servant's price with His life.

That shedding of His blood is what reconciles all to God (Colossians 1:20). In the body of Christ, "There is neither Jew nor Greek, there is neither slave nor free, there is neither male nor female; for you are all one in Christ Jesus" (Galatians 3:28). Zechariah prophesied this when he said, "Many nations shall be joined to the Lord in that day, and they shall become My people. And I will dwell in your midst. Then you will know that the Lord of hosts has sent Me to you" (Zechariah 2:11). This promise assures us that Christ's eternal kingdom will not only transcend earthly boundaries but also encompass all who seek His presence, uniting us as one.

Jesus Christ, our Emmanuel, came to dwell in our midst during His visible ministry, and He continues to come to us every time we receive His body and blood in the Lord's Supper for the forgiveness of our sins—a holy meal given to sustain us until His visible return.

Until that time, "Yes, all kings shall fall down before Him; all nations shall serve Him. For He will deliver the needy when he cries, the poor also, and him who has no helper. He will spare the poor and needy, and will save the souls of the needy. He will redeem their life from oppression and violence; and precious shall be their blood in His sight. And He shall live" (Psalm 72:11–15). It's comforting to know that, in spite of any worldly strife, Christ's reign is perfect.

The vision of the Lamb in His heavenly kingdom brings to mind Psalm 47:8–9: "God reigns over the nations; God sits on His holy throne. The princes of the people have gathered together, the people of the God of Abraham. For the shields of the earth belong to God; He is greatly exalted." These words have both a present and future fulfillment, because Jesus Christ is already Lord over the nations, and He rules over all creation as "the Alpha and the Omega, the Beginning and the End...who is and who was and who is to come, the Almighty" (Revelation 1:8).

Paul describes Christ's visible return as follows: "Then comes the end, when He delivers the kingdom to God the Father, when He puts an end to all rule and all authority and power. For He must reign till He has put all enemies under His feet. The last enemy that will be destroyed is death" (1 Corinthians 15:24–26). Once all death is destroyed at His coming, all will be bodily resurrected, as Job proclaimed: "For I know that my Redeemer lives, and He shall stand at last on the earth; and after my skin is destroyed, this I know, that in my flesh I shall see God, whom I shall see for myself, and my eyes shall behold, and not another. How my heart yearns within me!" (Job 19:25–27).

Yes, how our hearts yearn within us for that time to come!

God willing, the United States will remain strong until Jesus Christ returns. But if it doesn't, our eternal home with Him is secure, both now and forevermore.

May we remain faithful until the end.

Come, Lord Jesus!

Amen.

Prayer

Lord Jesus Christ, how we long for the day when You "will wipe away every tear from their eyes; there shall be no more death, nor sorrow, nor crying. There shall be no more pain, for the former things have passed away" (Revelation 21:4). What a glorious day that will be, when we'll experience perfect fellowship with You and each other. Until then, "let us hold fast the confession of our hope without wavering" (Hebrews 10:23), as we pray for our nation, its leaders, and its citizens. May You provide for and protect us until You return. Amen.

For Further Reflection

- Does it make you anxious to think of the United States ceasing to exist as a nation? Why or why not?
- How does anticipating Christ's eternal kingdom help you navigate life while we await his return?

Acknowledgments

To the One True God, Father, Son, and Holy Spirit. To the Father, for endlessly pursuing me, even when I was in full-blown rebellion. Thank You for never giving up on me. To Jesus Christ, for dying on the cross for my sins. Thank You for being my Lord and Savior. To the Holy Spirit, for interceding for me. Thank You for sustaining my faith.

To my husband. For twenty years, you've held my hand, dried my tears, laughed at my jokes (whether they were funny or not), and shown me what it means when a husband loves his wife like Christ loves the church. You're one of the most gifted theologians I've ever known, and it's an honor to learn at your feet, not only as your wife but also as a sheep in your flock. Thank you for sharing your vast knowledge of the Bible to improve this book, and for encouraging me when I felt unworthy of writing it.

To my children. Being your mother is such a blessing. Thank you for forgiving me when I fall short, and for loving me unconditionally. Watching you grow into the man and woman God created you to be is such a joy, and I pray that the country and world you inherit is more aligned with God's will.

To my in-laws. I never knew the sacrificial love of parents until you came into my life. As I often say, what God didn't give me through biology, He gave me through marriage. And a special shout-out to my brilliant, generous mother-in-law, who read this entire manuscript and applied her eagle eye to sharpen my writing.

To all of my brothers and sisters in Christ. Your fellowship and love mean more to me than words can express. Thank you to all who have prayed for me and with me, especially as I was writing this book. Your intercession made all the difference in the world.

To my friends and other family members. You know who you are. Thank you for being by my side in both bad times and good.

To the team at Post Hill Press. Thank you for stewarding this project so beautifully. I'm immensely grateful for all the time and effort you've invested in this book.

The grace of the Lord Jesus Christ, and the love of God,
and the communion of the Holy Spirit be with you all.
Amen.

—2 CORINTHIANS 13:14

About the Author

Amanda C. Bauch is a writer and editor whose creative nonfiction and short fiction have appeared both online and in print anthologies. As an editor, she has worked on well over a hundred books, including several bestsellers.

A first-generation college student, Amanda's the proud recipient of a Master of Fine Arts in creative writing from Lesley University in Cambridge, Massachusetts, and a Bachelor of Arts in English literature from Ithaca College in Ithaca, New York.

When she's not writing or editing—which is rarely—she usually can be found reading her Bible, hanging out with her family, listening to music, or snuggling with her cat, Phoebe.

Alongside her pastor-husband, she's raising a son and daughter in Nashville, Tennessee.